Leaving Early
Perspectives and Problems
in
Current Retirement Practice and Policy

Jeanne Prial Gordus

The University of Michigan

THE W.E. UPJOHN INSTITUTE FOR EMPLOYMENT RESEARCH

Library of Congress Cataloging in Publication Data

Gordus, Jeanne P
  Leaving early.

  Bibliography: p.
  1. Retirement age—United States.   2. Old age pensions—United States.   I. Title.
  HD7106.U6G67   331.25'2   80-39653
  ISBN 0-911558-78-0 (pbk.)

THE INSTITUTE, a nonprofit research organization, was established on July 1, 1945. It is an activity of the W. E. Upjohn Unemployment Trustee Corporation, which was formed in 1932 to administer a fund set aside by the late Dr. W. E. Upjohn for the purpose of carrying on "research into the causes and effects of unemployment and measures for the alleviation of unemployment."

The Author

Dr. Gordus is assistant research scientist with the Institute of Labor and Industrial Relations of The University of Michigan-Wayne State University. Her areas of research interest include unemployment, retirement, industrial relocation, and the social and psychological effects of economic change. She is co-editor of *Mental Health and the Economy* (1979) and author of *The Employment Relationship: Issues in Labor and Industrial Relations* (1979) and "Women in CETA: The Social Context of Public Service Employment" in D. McGuigan, ed., *Women's Life Cycle and Public Policy* (1980).

She received her M.A. and Ph.D. degrees in economic history from The University of Michigan.

For my husband, Don

Acknowledgments

This work was made possible by a grant from the W. E. Upjohn Institute for Employment Research. The assistance of the Institute's director, Dr. E. Earl Wright, and its editor, Judith Brawer, is gratefully acknowledged.

Staff members at the Research Division of the Institute of Labor and Industrial Relations, The University of Michigan-Wayne State University, were helpful. The research Division co-director, Dr. Louis A. Ferman, provided valuable support at critical junctures. Research assistance was provided by Michelle Faunce and James M. Rehmus. The contribution to this work by Paul Jarley was important, and the assistance of Gregory Langworthy is also appreciated.

Professor Stanley E. Seashore read a draft of the manuscript and made valuable comments. Dr. Harold L. Sheppard provided advice, suggestions, and constructive criticism, and I am especially grateful to him. These colleagues and associates deserve full credit for their contributions. All blame, however, belongs solely to the author.

Foreword

The trend toward early retirement has emerged as a key public policy question which has implications for individual workers, employers, and the national economy. As noted in this study, persons who elect to retire early include a vast array of workers. Early retirees range from persons who leave the labor force involuntarily for health and unemployment reasons to individuals whose pension benefits and private investments will allow them to "retire" well in advance of the traditional retirement age.

The primary purpose of this monograph is a review of existing research and literature on the early retirement phenomenon. Dr. Gordus assesses the benefits and costs of early retirement from several perspectives and considers the implications of early retirement for future research and public policy.

Facts and observations expressed in the study are the sole responsibility of the author. Her viewpoints do not necessarily represent positions of the W.E. Upjohn Institute for Employment Research.

E. Earl Wright
Director

Kalamazoo, Michigan
November 1980

CONTENTS

Introduction

Early retirement, a term once susceptible to simple definition, is in fact a phrase which describes different kinds of detachments from the labor force of individuals at ages earlier than had once been arbitrarily determined as normal, that is 65 years of age. Less than two decades ago, an early retiree was a person who chose to leave the labor force before 65 years of age, usually between 62 and 64 years of age. At present, because of increasingly liberal benefits as well as decreasingly rigid criteria for eligibility, that definition no longer holds. Instead, there is now an array of individuals who have retired early. At one end of such an idealized array are affluent persons in their mid or early 50s whose pension benefits and private investments or other income permit them to pursue lives in which either leisure, community service, or second careers are relatively well-subsidized. At the other end of such an array are persons who are, for all practical purposes, unemployed and becoming increasingly unemployable, but who differ from the long term older unemployed persons of previous decades by virtue of the source of the income which they now have—early retirement pension benefits.

This study of early retirement was undertaken as an effort to draw together what is known about this new phenomenon from materials already developed on the subject. The purposes of such a review were not strictly theoretical. For one thing, the study began at a time when it appeared that public pressures were producing a situation which was paradoxical. Early retirement had been enshrined, for some at least, with those long sought and hard won benefits—medical coverage, workers' compensation, and pension benefits of all kinds—which help assure a decent working and post-working life. But at the same time, legislation had finally been passed to raise mandatory retirement age from 65 to 70 in many establishments and occupations. These countercurrents are more than just another example of disagreement about issues of public policy. They both express and act upon concerns and serious reservations about early retirement as an appropriate method of labor force reduction at a time when it is not clear whether early retirement benefits all who take it and when the continuing state of constriction of the nation's retirement resources is already worsening. In fact, it is possible that these resources could become drastically reduced in another two decades because of demographic pressure alone, and perhaps even completely exhausted should the trend toward early retirement continue at its present level.

The aging of societies and the problems of retirement are very modern phenomena. In the course of human history, only a handful of persons could expect to reach the normal span of life, 70 or more years, before death. A vast majority failed to reach 35 years of age. Not until the nineteenth century did sufficient numbers of persons live long enough to make age or aging, or the support of the aging, a problem suitable for public intervention. In the late nineteenth century, retirement had begun. Poverty among elderly Americans had always been a problem, but as more Americans survived to older ages and more of them withdrew from the labor force, the problem became more severe and widespread. Private pension plans were developed

gradually, and with the enactment of social security legislation, the threat of poverty to older Americans who were no
longer working was reduced. The extensions of these arrangements to provide options and incentives for Americans
to retire early—not just after years earlier than 65, but as
early as 55—took place much more rapidly. This development in labor force policy could have substantial impact on
the economic system, the social structure and individual lives
in the coming decades.

As the second chapter of this study emphasizes, when the
option to retire early had developed, it became clear that not
all persons availed themselves of this opportunity. If, in fact,
early retirement is not as advantageous to proper deploy-
ment of the American labor force as once commonly held, it
was important to know who chose this detachment from the
world of work and who delayed retirement. In general, some
tentative answers can be provided to that question. Involuntary early retirement is closely associated with prolonged
unemployment or declining health. Voluntary early retirement is associated with favorable postretirement income prospects, good health, and substantial planning preparation
for the retirement experience. Some early retirements are
more difficult to categorize and seem to result from the
availability of benefits, some pressure from employers, and a
perceived lack of reward from the work role.

The third chapter of this study begins with individual
issues. The individual experience is an essential element for
investigation because certainly how retirement is perceived
by those presently in that state will have some impact on
those who decide in the future. The specific methods, as well
as the conceptual bias brought to the retirement experience
by those who have studied it, provide a source of confusion
as well as enlightenment, but it is clear that those who have
retired early with sufficient resources and good health and
who chose to do so, experience retirement as a beneficial ar-

rangement which probably even prolongs life. Those not so favored may find early retirement better than unemployment or unsubsidized disability, but the experience is radically different from and much less fulfilling than that of their more favored cohorts. As the third chapter demonstrates, there are social consequences—and ultimately policy issues—involved with individual retirement experience. For example, social service systems and adult and higher education in America have begun to focus on older Americans as a population to be served, in some instances transferring their function from a younger dependent population to another population which happens to be older.

The final chapter considers implications for future research and public policy. If, as many assert, the nation's retirement resources will be subject to burdens which it cannot sustain within the next two decades, a reconsideration of early retirement policies is essential. While such a reconsideration may arise from concern over whether the nation can afford maintained or increased levels of early withdrawal from the labor force, it must proceed from information about how the early retirement decision is made and how the experience is perceived. Early retirement, for those who are financially secure and healthy and who plan for this stage in their life cycle, is a thoughtful decision and a positive experience. Early retirement can also be beneficial for those whose health is deteriorating, but it is possible that early retirement for these persons is simply another type of extended and perhaps liberalized disability. Other involuntary early retirees, those whose employment histories have been troubled, might be assisted by policies directed toward retaining them in the work force in some capacity. Still other early retirees do not make a truly voluntary decision and may not experience retirement positively. They have responded to a mixture of liberalized benefits, job dissatisfaction, a perceived lack of employment-related rewards, and pressure from employers and coworkers. If that is the case for some workers, and this literature review indicates that it is, the focus for research and policy should extend beyond incentives and disincentives or early retirement to include the employment problems of older workers.

Chapter 1
Aging, Work and Retirement
in Perspective

The normal limit of age has not changed very much throughout most of human history. The Old Testament notion of three score and ten has not been extended significantly over the intervening millenia. However, although some individuals lived to a ripe age, normal life span for thousands of years was much shorter, perhaps 25 or 30 years at most. A short life span for most individuals and a low median age for populations were characteristic of most human societies until quite recently. Under such conditions, withdrawal from the labor force in the later years was simply not an option for most people since so few survived beyond what is now considered early middle age. The great demographic change of the eighteenth and nineteenth centuries throughout the Western World was the survival of more individuals, not the extension of the normal limit of life. Under these circumstances, the median age of populations rose, and more individuals survived to old age and could retire.[1]

When the first census was taken in America in 1790, the median age of white males was just 16 years of age, in con-

1. Sherburne Cook, "Aging of and in Populations," in P.S. Timiras, ed., *Development Physiology and Aging* (New York, 1972), p. 595.

trast to the median age of males and females in the 1970s which is about 30 years of age. The changing median age of the American population is shown in table 1-1. In 1790, less than 2 percent of the population were 65 years of age or older; in the Bicentennial year, about 10 percent of the population had reached that age. The demographic shape of American society changed little until about 1820 and retirement was not common. Most people continued to work until death.

The Decline of Labor Force Participation of Older American Men

By 1870, as table 1-2 shows, about 20 percent of the men 65 years and over had withdrawn from the labor force.[2] Retirement during this period was not a result of economic incentives to the potential retirees; the late nineteenth and early twentieth century was a period in which poverty and old age were intimately associated in America. During the first decades of the twentieth century, problems of old age, a state now reached by many, were perceived as problems and as a proper area for government intervention. The several states took the initiative, Massachusetts with the first commission on aging in 1909 and Arizona with the first state old age pension system, and the federal government witnessed the introduction of the first federal old age pension bill, but not by any means the last.[3] The struggle to establish a financial floor below which the income of no older American could fall had begun in public conciousness with the publication of an article by Edward Everett Hale, Chaplain to the United States Senate, in which he proposed an annuity

---

2. Dominic Gagliardo, *American Social Insurance* (New York, 1955); U.S. Bureau of Economic Analysis, *Long Term Economic Growth* (Washington, 1973), pp. 212-214.

3. Lee W. Squier, *Old Age Dependency in the United States* (New York, 1912), pp. 6-14; Abraham Epstein, *Facing Old Age: A Study of Old Age Dependency in the United States and Old Age Pensions* (New York, 1922), pp. 20-27.

Table 1-1
The Changing Age Composition of the American Population, Median Age, 1790-1975

	TOTAL			WHITE			NON-WHITE		
	Male	Female	Total	Male	Female	Total	Male	Female	Total
U.S. 1790				15.9	16.3	16.0			
1800				15.7	16.1	16.0			
1810				15.9					
1820	16.6	16.7	16.7	16.5	16.6	16.5	16.9	17.4	17.2
1830	17.1	17.3	17.2	17.2	17.3	17.2	16.7	17.1	16.9
1840	17.8	17.7	17.8	17.9	17.8	17.9	17.0	17.5	17.3
1850	19.2	18.6	18.9	19.5	18.8	19.2	17.3	17.4	17.4
1860	19.8	19.1	19.4	20.2	19.3	19.7	17.5	17.5	17.5
1870	20.2	20.1	20.2	20.6	20.3	20.4	18.2	18.9	18.5
1880	21.2	20.7	20.9	21.6	21.1	21.4	17.9	18.0	18.0
1890	22.3	21.6	22.0	22.9	22.1	22.5	18.5	18.3	18.4
1900	23.3	22.4	22.9	23.8	22.9	23.4	20.0	19.5	19.7
1910	24.6	23.5	24.1	24.9	23.9	24.5	21.5	20.6	21.1
1920	25.8	24.7	25.3	26.1	25.1	25.6	23.1	21.9	22.4
1930	26.7	26.2	26.5	27.1	26.6	26.9	23.9	23.1	23.5
1940	29.1	29.0	29.0	29.5	29.5	29.5	25.4	25.1	25.2
1950	29.9	30.5	30.2	30.4	31.1	30.8	25.9	26.2	26.1
1960	28.7	30.3	29.5	29.4	31.1	30.3	22.7	24.3	23.5
1970	26.8	29.3	28.1	27.6	30.2	28.9	21.5	23.8	22.7
1975			28.7			29.5			23.2

SOURCE: Historical Statistics of the United States, Series A 86-94; *Statistical Abstract of the U.S.*, 1978, Chart 26, p. 26.

system because as he said "there is now no place in our working order for older men."[4]

Table 1-2
Labor Force Participation of Males 65 and Over

Year	Percent of males 65 and over gainfully employed (Gagliardo)	Labor force participation rates, males 65 and over (Census)
1870	80.6	--
1880	76.7	--
1890	73.8	68.3
1900	68.4	63.1
1910	63.7	--
1920	60.2	55.6
1930	58.3	54.0
1940	41.5	44.2
1950	48.4	45.8
1960	--	33.1
1970	--	26.8

Source: Dominic Gagliardo, *American Social Insurance* (New York, 1955), p. 32; U.S. Bureau of Economic Analysis, *Long Term Economic Growth* (Washington, 1973), pp. 212-214.

If there was not place for the aging in the work force, what economic resources did exist in those early years when there was retirement of a sort but no federal old age pension schemes, virtually no private or union pension plans, and few takers for the annuity programs offered by some insurance companies? A survey of the post-65 population in Massachusetts in 1930 assigned only 23 percent of the older population to dependency status, and most of that fraction were persons institutionalized in prisons, hospitals, or almshouses or taking part in some of the relief programs. But, as the report stated, no account was taken of church,

4. Edward Everett Hale, "Old Age Pensions," *Cosmopolitan 35,* pp. 168-169.

society or settlement house assistance to these older persons, and no contribution to their resources from friends or families was considered to place them in "dependent" status. Only paupers, and the term was used to describe the indigent institutionalized, were dependent for financial reasons alone.[5]

The relatively leisurely pace at which national pension plans developed and were implemented reflected a sense within American society that older persons ought to have saved during their working lives. According to at least one authority, for more than a century the lower two-thirds of the American population has had zero savings.[6] Annuity plans, popular abroad, have, for a variety of reasons, not been particularly successful in America.[7]

Only a minority of those who retired in the late nineteenth century could expect to subsist on savings or annuities. Most retirees depended on some form of assistance about which little information has survived—private philanthropic societies, churches, other voluntary groups and, probably most important, other members of the family. Therefore, for this particular dependent population, the mechanisms for transferring resources were informal and voluntary and not subject to monitoring or control. Indeed, it is likely that, in many cases, where children or other relatives refused to contribute to the support of indigent elders, no stronger incentive than the approval of other family members and friends was provided by society to those who contributed these resources.[8]

5. Squier, *Old Age Dependency,* p. 6.

6. Gabriel Kolko, *Wealth and Power in America* (New York, 1962), pp. 48-51.

7. David Hackett Fischer, *Growing Old in America* (Oxford, England, 1978), p. 272.

8. Ibid., p. 273.

The Development of Retirement Resource Systems

The first incursion into this informal, *ad hoc,* retirement resource system was made by private companies. After the American Express Company led the way in 1875, other companies, especially the railroads followed and the specific financial arrangement commonly made by these companies came to be called the "railroad formula," which was a pension figured on the basis of 1 percent of a worker's annual wage multiplied by his years of service. While the formula for benefits was similar among the railroads, the age favored for retirement varied between 65 and 70, with 70 usually the mandatory age. The first thrust of private pension plan development occurred in an industry which was highly profitable and which employed some highly skilled workers who were already organized, for example, the Brotherhood of Locomotive Engineers. There are clearly preconditions which are necessary for the development of any worker benefit arrangement and in the case of the railroads around the closing years of the nineteenth century and the beginning of the twentieth century these necessary conditions existed: a generally prosperous economy in which one type of industry was particularly successful and profitable, and a combination of skill, sophistication and power among workers in those industries.[9]

Pension plans were also adopted by craft unions on their own initiative, but growth in the pension support for retired persons continued to occur in private industry as major companies—Standard Oil, Armour, Du Pont, John Deere, International Harvester, Procter and Gamble, Western Electric, and Westinghouse—developed their own retirement schemes, often based on the "railroad formula." Those

---

9. Nathan Schock, *Trends in Gerontology* (Stanford, 1951).

whose retirements were subsidized by private pension plans were not supported lavishly by any means, but in contrast to those whose detachment from the labor force was not accompanied by pension payments, participants in private pension plans were relatively secure from economic deprivation. However, the security was only apparent. Most private pensions were not a right in the sense that they were the inalienable possession of the workers after a specified period; there were no contractual rights to pension or payment. Government workers on every level were either without pension plans or were included in meager plans in the few American cities having such arrangements for their workers.[10] As one worker commented, horses, in this case an artillery horse, retired assured of full support until death, while he, a postal employee for 50 years, had no postretirement benefits at all.[11]

But the federal government, while not providing retirement benefits for its workers, had been in the habit of paying a kind of pension even since 1866. It is a little difficult to explain how, by the year 1905, there could have been nearly 1,000,000 veterans receiving pensions. The Spanish American War provided the country with few veterans. The Southern states cared for their own veterans after the Civil War, and the Union Army had fewer than 1,100,000 active participants in 1865. The degree to which veterans' benefits actually functioned for some as old age pensions will not be clear until a close study of the records is made, but it is amply clear that this vast dependent population made a significant dent in the federal budget, accounting for 40 percent of total expenditures in some years.[12] By the turn of the century, and until after World War I, a significant number of

10. Fischer, *Growing Old in America,* pp. 170-172.

11. D.D. Cowgill, "The Aging of Populations and Societies," *Annals of the American Academy of Political and Social Science 415* (1974), p. 7.

12. Fischer, *Growing Old in America,* p. 273.

older Americans were supported by these benefits, since they extended to the survivors of decreased servicemen. Several social groups were excluded from this quasi-pension plan: blacks, women without demonstrated relationships to veterans, and new immigrants, as well as the urban poor.

As those who claimed veteran status and their dependents died, the only supported retirees outside almshouses were those with private pension benefits and those in the public sector to whom such benefits were gradually extended. The debate about old age insurance began to develop in the years before World War I and it intensified as poverty became endemic among older Americans. Dependency upon almshouses or charity among the elderly grew alarmingly as eligibility for veterans' benefits declined among the older population, as more poor Americans lived longer, and as society became more industrialized and urbanized and included large numbers of people who had virtually no family in this country. In 1910, about 23 percent of the old were dependent in this sense; in 1922, before the Depression, dependency had increased to about 33 percent. In 1930, the rate was 40 percent; in 1935, 50 percent and by 1940 about 65 percent of the elderly were dependent.[13] Obviously the disastrous poverty among the aged was exacerbated by the Depression and fewer formal and informal sources of retirement income were available, despite the enactment of old age pensions by several states. By 1937, even after the development of many private pension plans, only 5 percent of the elderly were enjoying the old age benefits of them.[14]

The development of numerous movements devoted to the passage and implementation of national old age insurance and pension benefits in America, similar to those schemes long in use in Europe, has been studied from many perspec-

13. Ibid., pp. 272, 275-277.

14. M.S. Shearon, "Economic Status of the Aged," *Social Security Bulletin* (March 1938), p. 6.

tives. While only students of American social movements or the development of pensions may now be concerned with all these movements, one of them, the Townsend movement, survives in the form of a classic case study in organizational decline.[15] The economic implications of social security legislation have been the object of many studies, and accounts of the ideological and political currents which obstructed or facilitated passage of social security legislation are available in several first-rate studies.[16]

The first movement toward supporting retirement through private pension plans for the elderly began in the last quarter of the nineteenth century and gathered force thereafter. That such resources were insufficient for the entire growing group of elderly Americans became obvious throughout the early twentieth century, and the growing poverty of older persons in the midst of general economic distress finally was alleviated by federal intervention. With a pause for World War II, the drive continued toward increasing coverage for American workers through private pension schemes combined with consistent improvement of social security coverage. Table 1-3 shows the increase both in numbers of private pension plans and in numbers of workers covered by such plans from 1875 to 1970.

---

15. David Sills, *The Volunteers* (Glencoe, IL, 1958), pp. 253-268.
16. Fischer, *Growing Old in America,* pp. 157-195; 246-264.

Table 1-3
Growth in Private Pension Plans 1875-1970

Year	Number of plans	Number of workers covered (millions)
1875	1	n.a.
1900	12	n.a.
1920	270	n.a.
1930	720	2.4
1935	1,090	2.6
1940	1,965	3.7
1945	7,425	5.6
1950	12,330	9.8
1955	23,000	15.4
1960	n.a.	21.2
1965	n.a.	25.3
1970	n.a.	29.7

Source: U.S. Department of Labor, *Digest of Selected Pension Plans 1976-78* (Washington, 1979).

Note: n.a. = not available. Emphasis has been placed upon numbers of workers covered from 1960 in, for example, *Digest of Selected Pension Plans* and other standard compilations, not on the number of plans.

Summary

In 1870, about 20 percent of the males 65 years of age and over were retired. In 1970, nearly 75 percent of the male population over 65 had withdrawn from the labor force. This trend toward retirement reflects a demographic shift, a rising average age at death. The incomes of retired Americans are now maintained through benefits from private pension plans and from social security benefits. For over a century, demographic change and the gradual development of pension benefits have combined to produce a relatively new phenomenon, retirement. More recently, the extension of pension benefits to those younger than 65, in combination with other factors, has produced an even newer phenomenon, early retirement.

Chapter 2
The Early Retirement Option: Economic Policies and Individual Decisions

The rapid growth of early retirement benefits and the increasingly liberal criteria for qualification for early retirement over the past several decades is the subject of the first part of this chapter. The focus of the second part is the early retirement decision. It is clear that the availability of the early retirement option has been beneficial to persons whose health makes working difficult or impossible and to those whose jobs have been eliminated by catastrophic unemployment. However, these persons retire involuntarily. Studies of the early retirement decision indicate that early retirement benefits and liberal eligibility criteria are closely associated with the voluntary early retirement decision. There are still other workers for whom factors such as supervisory and peer pressure and weakened attachment to the work force are significantly associated with a decision to retire early—a decision which is neither involuntary nor completely voluntary.

In general, individual decisions to retire early are based in part upon the availability of resources for retirement. These resources can include individual savings and investments, but the basic component of financial support for the early retiree and his or her dependents is usually a pension with early retirement provision. Social Security payments are directly significant only later in the early retiree's post-retirement life. Another potentially important economic factor influencing individual decisions is the individual's history of investment and obligation. Clearly those whose children are grown, educated and attached to the labor force and whose major lifetime purchases, such as a house, have been completed, are in a better position to retire with security than those whose histories of investment and obligation are still in a less advantageous state. Still, for most, the availability of private pension support subsequent to an early retirement decision is crucial.

The Growth of Private Pensions

The American experience, at the turn of the century, in supporting older Americans no longer in the labor force, manifested a pattern in which private industry took the lead, with close involvement from important groups in organized labor (for example, the railroads and the Brotherhood of Locomotive Engineers). The development of early retirement follows a similar outline.

A study done under the auspices of the Social Security Administration in 1974[1] reviewed the status of private pension plans at that point, which was, as the author noted, a convenient milestone year because of the passage of the Employee Retirement Income Security Act (ERISA) which marks the beginning of a new era in private pension development. In fact, since the implementation of ERISA began in January 1976, the major concern about private pensions has not been their expansion but their rearrangement to conform to the federal standards of vesting, funding, and participation, devised to provide greater assurance that employees would indeed benefit from those pensions they had expected.

1. Alfred M. Skolnik, "Private Pension Plans 1950-1974," *Social Security Bulletin* (June 1976), pp. 3-14.

In 1974, about 30 million workers were participants in private pension plans, and of these about half, or 15 million workers, participated in plans which had been negotiated under collective bargaining agreements. Of those workers belonging to negotiated plans, about half, or 8 million workers, belonged to multiemployer plans. This membership in collectively-bargained multiemployer plans in 1974 is an enormous change from the beginning of the period, 1950, when fewer than a million workers could retain their pensions while moving from one employer to another. Such arrangements are now, in contrast, often industry-wide. Before the implementation of ERISA, only about one-third of the employees covered in private pension plans had coverage that was insured. Nearly all the multiemployer plans at that time were noninsured, as were union-financed plans and a whole range of unfunded plans.

While the increase in participation and coverage has been substantial, the percentage increase in beneficiaries receiving payment has been even greater. In 1950, about 450,000 persons drew benefits, compared with about 6,390,000 in 1974, an increase of 1480 percent. This, of course, is in sharp contrast to the increase in coverage which was about 800 percent over the same period. Therefore, in private pension plans, the same demographic pressures are obvious as those apparent in the public sector; the ratio of worker to beneficiary changed from a twenty-workers-to-one beneficiary ratio to a five-workers-to-one beneficiary ratio, although these ratios do not have the same significance for annuity or other insured and invested pension schemes as they do for pay-as-you-go plans. Part of the pattern of increase in beneficiaries, particularly in the latter part of the 1960s and early 1970s, is due to early retirement and the increasing liberalization of benefits and early retirement age and service requirements.[2]

2. Evan L. Hodgens, "Key Changes in Major Pension Plans," *Monthly Labor Review* July 1975), pp. 22-27.

The Developmenmt of the
Early Retirement Benefit

The story of early retirement benefits and their extraordinary growth and development begins a little later than 1950 although, as many have remarked, early retirement was already prevalent. Lenore Epstein, in one of the first studies of early retirement makes the following observations documented by Social Security Administration earnings:

— men who had elected to begin drawing social security benefits at age 62 were only half as likely as age 65 retirees to have had covered earnings of $4,800 in the year with the largest earnings; and

— early retirees "were almost four times as likely to have earned less than $2,400 in their best year since 1950."[3]

Early retirement, as recently as 1966, had negative connotations and was associated with chronic unemployment, obsolescence of job skills, low earnings, and a lack of interest in working. Workers exhibiting such characteristics would likely have been considered appropriate candidates for early retirement by management.[4]

But the focus was not exclusively upon those whom management wished to retire individually; the implementation of early retirement programs on such a broad scale was, to some extent, a considered decision on the part of many sectors of management in an effort to manipulate the labor force in order to secure high productivity. Organized labor had experienced, in the postwar period, several setbacks as plants closed and relocated, or simply closed, often leaving

---

3. Lenore A. Epstein, "Early Retirement and Work-Life Experience," *Social Security Bulletin* (March 1966), p. 3.

4. Richard Barfield and James Morgan, *Early Retirement: The Decision and the Experience* (Ann Arbor, 1969), p. 4.

older workers unwilling to move and unable to secure employment of a similar kind and remuneration level, to a fate which was in effect, early retirement, but an unprotected early retirement.[5] Moreover, the several kinds of industrial, technical and organizational change usually classified together and called technological changes (including plant closing and relocations) threatened older workers disproportionately, thus indirectly favoring younger employees. To some degree, therefore, the concerted effort to secure good early retirement benefits for workers by their representatives in organized labor was simply a response to management initiatives and a method for offsetting planned layoffs and for minimizing the possibility of new and disruptive management methods for reducing the work force. At the same time, the historical bias toward younger workers with their alleged propensity for greater productivity, a bias already more than a century old, was given additional impetus by the sheer numbers of young persons attempting to enter the labor force especially during the 1960s. Early retirement benefits became an important bargaining issue as labor unions moved to protect potentially endangered older members while helping secure entry positions for younger workers and new union members.

Changing Patterns in Early Retirement Provisions

Contrasts are striking from 1960 through the mid-1970s. The Bureau of Labor Statistics reported after a review of the pension plans whose specific arrangements were disclosed under the Welfare and Pension Plans Disclosure Act, that the proportion of employees covered by early retirement pro-

---

5. See, for example, the conclusions and the summary of such cases in William Haber, Louis A. Ferman, and John Hudson, *The Impact of Technological Change: The American Experience* (Kalamazoo, 1963), pp. 47 ff.

visions under such plans increased from 23 percent in 1962 to more than 90 percent in 1971.[6] In addition, the locus of control over the early retirement decision was transferred from management to individual employees. In the 1950s, 60 percent of the plans having early retirement provisions made the approval of management essential to an employee's retiring early. By 1971, about half the covered workers would have been required to seek company approval. A recent Banker's Trust Company Study, quoted by Skolnik,[7] indicates that in 1974 only 12 percent of the conventional plans with early retirement provisions required company approval and only 4 percent of the so-called pattern plans included this requirement. The difference between conventional and pattern pension plans is that pattern plans, usually negotiated between international unions and certain companies or groups of companies, base pension payment on sums which vary with years of service but do not reflect differences among workers in wage or salary rates. Conventional plans are usually, though not always, non-negotiated, and pension payments reflect *both* compensation *and* years of service.

To qualify for early retirement, it has usually been necessary to attain a certain age and to have attained a specific number of years of service. Some conventional plans, specifically those not collectively bargained, have depended upon an age attainment only. But service requirements have become increasingly important as a criterion for early retirement benefits. The "30-and-out" plan, for example, has been successful in the automobile industry as well as many other manufacturing and fabricating industries. The shift in emphasis on length of service has often been balanced with a lower age requirement.[8] If

---

6. Hodgens, "Key Changes in Pension Plans," pp. 25-26.

7. Skolnik, "Private Pension Plans," pp. 3-11.

8. Harry E. Davis, "Multiemployer Pension Plan Provisions in 1973," *Monthly Labor Review* (October 1974), pp. 10-16.

30-and-out was a phase with a magic number in it, an even more magic number has emerged from the ever-increasing availability of early retirement benefits—age 55. The normal rhythm of American, and for that matter most Western and socialist, working lives has allowed for a period of early dependency and education, lasting from 18 to 25 years (excluding lengthy professional preparation) followed by a working period of at least 40 years culminating in a period of leisure with security until death. But just as death is occurring at a later age for more persons, more workers are provided powerful incentives in the form of financial security to prolong dependency in later life by entering upon that phase earlier and departing from it later.

Early Retirement Clauses

The *Digest of Selected Pension Plans, 1976-78,* provides information about 141 major pension plans.[9] Of these collectively bargained, multiemployer plans, 135 had early retirement clauses. The average age requirement for early retirement was 56.61 years, with 62 years of age as the oldest age at which retirement was considered early. The average service requirement for these plans was 10.74 years, with some plans having a service requirement of 25 years. Some plans (14 or 10.3 percent) had a specific 30-and-out provision. Only four of these plans indicated that management approval was required, just 2.9 percent.

The benefits for early retirement have normally been at a rate lower than the prevailing rate for normal retirement, and initially such reductions were calculated on the basis of an actuarial formula developed to compensate for the longer period of retirement expected for early retirees. It has been noted that as late as 1969, 48 percent of the pattern plans and

---

9. U.S. Department of Labor, *Digest of Selected Pension Plans, 1976-78,* with Supplement (Washington, 1979).

53 percent of the conventional plans paid only the actuarially reduced amount to early retirees. However, in the pattern plans, as a result of negotiated settlements over the past decade, a shift has occurred and many are now paying full accrued pension benefits to early retirees, a result of the heavy emphasis on 30-and-out issues in collective bargaining in the early 1970s.[10]

Special Early Retirement Clauses

Some pattern plans interlock with the Social Security system, providing special benefits to age 62 for early (pre-62) retirees with a provision for reducing these special benefits when Social Security payments begin. Actually this particular variant developed in the early 1960s and has not been extended significantly since then. Special early retirement benefits and the clauses defining them were negotiated widely in the 1960s; in most cases this special arrangement provides for double the normal benefits from the time of early retirement until the age of normal retirement.

Returning again to the *Digest of Selected Pension Plans, 1976-78* for a review of the special benefit clauses, it is noteworthy that considerable control, in both the form of requirements for management approval, as well as the right to retire some individuals involuntarily, is retained by management. Of the 135 plans, 25 had a special early retirement clause.[11] The average age requirement was 56.15 years, with all these clauses having an age requirement ranging narrowly from 55 to 60 years. The average service requirement for special early retirement benefits was 11.7 years, ranging from 10 to 20 years of service. Of the 25 plans, 64 percent, or

10. Harry E. Davis, "Pension Provisions Affecting the Employment of Older Workers," *Monthly Labor Review* (November 1975), pp. 41-45.

11. *Digest of Selected Pension Plans, 1976-78.*

16, required management approval for an individual to have special early retirement benefits, and 20 percent (5 out of 25) included a provision in which management could retire a worker involuntarily.

Clearly such liberal benefits are highly likely, if not specifically intended, to encourage the retirement of older workers so as to prevent layoffs. In this case, as in others, efforts to balance the interests of industry and labor in the development of pension benefits tend to balance the interests of younger and older workers. Younger, more recently hired workers are those most likely to be laid off and early retirement provisions provide incentives for older workers to depart, thereby increasing the chances that younger workers will not be laid off at all and also providing those younger workers with the seniority, comparatively speaking, that they had not had previous to the retirement of older co-workers. Such arrangements highlight intergenerational rights and provileges, while exacerbating intergenerational tensions. During those rounds of bargaining, particularly between the United Automobile Workers and the major auto manufacturers, rank-and-file members consistently comment that while it is necessary to provide inflation protection for retirees, such priorities during bargaining may operate to the disadvantage of presently employed workers. At present, both the absolute numbers as well as the percentage of such retirees is larger than previously, although it is a considerably more modest percentage than can be expected in twenty years if current trends toward early retirement continue at present levels. In two decades, therefore, both the actual pressure as well as the perceived pressure upon union workers *versus* retirees can be expected to increase. While such industry-specific problems differ from the broader national prospect, the same trends could generate the same perceptions, pressures, and tensions.

Vesting Rights

Consideration of vesting rights for pension plans will clarify the advantages to industry of early retirement. Turning once again to the *Digest of Selected Pension Plans, 1978-78,* the following profile can be discerned.[12]

All plans gave total vesting rights after some period of time and service, and sometimes after attainment of a specified age. Nearly all the plans required ten years of service, although the average service requirement among 135 plans was 9.72 years. Some plans, 16 (or 11.85 percent), had both age and service rquirements and the average age requirement was 53.56 years. These vesting arrangements are designed to comply with the provisions of ERISA, and thus protect the retirement benefits of employees.

Some Costs and Benefits of Early Retirement

The advantage of providing powerful incentives to employees who are at the top end of the pay scale to retire twenty years or so after they acquire total vesting rights and a decade or more earlier than usual is that early retirement can be much less expensive than the retention of an unproductive highly-paid employee. To pension off an early retiree is not very expensive when the cost is actuarially reduced.

The funding of pensions is deductible for corporate tax purposes. The maximum amount which can be expensed is the normal cost plus 10 percent of the unfunded past service cost balance plus or minus an interest equivalent on any difference between the amounts expensed and the amounts

---

12. Ibid.

funded. Given a corporate tax rate of 46 percent, the real cost of any pension is only 54 percent of the total shown since the other 46 percent is funded in what would otherwise be taxes. Further, since pensions are often annuities, their cost to management is not the benefits paid the retirees over the period of retirement but the amount paid years before to insure that payment subsequent to the employee's retirement; such costs to the employer may be even lower. Obviously part of the costs for early retirement are borne by the taxpayer, and the tax structure provides an incentive to management to retire expensive and possible unproductive workers early.[13]

Involuntary Early Retirees

Leaving aside for a moment the question of whether the increase in early retirements generally is desirable for individuals or the economy, two groups of individuals, loosely described and defined, are clearly assisted enormously by the development of early retirement options. Those who have become disabled, to the point where work is difficult, have been adequately provided with retirement resources through such pension plans with a combination of disability and early retirement clauses. The other group, older workers caught in a catastrophic unemployment situation, are clearly advantaged. Such workers, firmly ensconced in their community and reluctant to leave, often unwilling and unable to train for new types of work which might not even exist, fare much better now than, for example, those who were caught in the Packard Motor Car closing some years ago. In the Aiken,

---

13. This can be calculated for specific employment situations from data available in *The Economic Aspects of Pensions: A Summary Report,* National Bureau of Economic Research (1968).

Ferman, and Sheppard study of 260 of these workers it was observed that:

> . . . the respondents averaged slightly more than ten months of joblessness in the twenty-seven month postshutdown period studied. Only 45 percent of the sample was actually reemployed at the time of the interview; 23 percent had never found a job and 32 percent had found and lost at least one job.

> Age, rather than education or skill levels, was the most important factor in the number of months of unemployment. Workers over sixty years of age averaged almost fifteen months without work. Age was also the strongest factor relating to job mobility. Education and job mobility were also closely related, and among the reemployed workers those with better education were most likely to be receiving wages comparable with their previous earnings at Packard.[14]

Most important, 60 of the 305 Packard workers had never been reemployed from the closing until the time of the study, and age was the most powerful predictor of problems associated with lengths of time until reemployment as well as eventual nonemployment. Such findings are dramatic, but other studies demonstrate precisely the same trends, different perhaps in detail but generally similar. Early retirement provisions protect older workers caught in such situations from the severe economic deprivation encountered by the Packard workers and can only be counted as a new and important advantage to this group of involuntarily unemployed persons. Equally clear is the motivation of organized labor to protect such groups of members and the consequent bargaining for liberalization of early retirement benefits and requirements.

---

14. Michael Aiken, Louis A. Ferman, and H.L. Sheppard, *Economic Failure, Alienation, and Extremism* (Ann Arbor, 1968), pp. 31-50.

Both these loosely defined groups, the disabled and the involuntarily jobless through catastrophic unemployment, have few options. They do not select early retirement as an option in the same sense those who remain functionally healthy and whose jobs are not seriously threatened are free to do. Consequently, it is important to look at the retirement decision and its determinants for those whose options are open. Policies developed to encourage or discourage early retirement will inevitably and necessarily be designed for those who choose to retire early freely, without necessity or constraint.

Choosing to Retire Early

To some degree, the preceding discussion departs from the perspective adopted by those who did the landmark studies in early retirement. Rather than assuming that the availability of and increasingly liberal benefits and eligibility requirements for pensions were necessary conditions for the early retirement decision in most cases, the object of early studies was to determine *if* workers would indeed respond to this incentive. The study which is still the standard in the field was done in the early 1960s and published in 1969. It was designed, among other things, to test the hypothesis that increased levels of early retirement benefits would be an incentive to potential retirees.[15] It is easy, a decade or more after the appearance of this study, to examine the instrument, the conceptual basis of this study, or the population studied, and note that more extensive questioning on one or another issue would have been helpful, or that other concerns or other groups might have provided important information. However, the quality of this study and the influence its findings have had could hardly have been greater. The work of Barfield and Morgan in this study, and in later

---

15. Barfield and Morgan, *Early Retirement.*

ies, is still the basis of most of what is known
ensions of early retirement: the decision to
ostretirement experience.

…or objective of the Barfield and Morgan research
…as to identify the factors that influence the early retirement
decision. To do this, a double-tiered analysis was done in
which data drawn from a nationwide random survey of
working and retired Americans were arrayed beside data
from a second survey of working and retired UAW
members. The most important factors affecting the decision
for early retirement were found to be financial. The
strongest correlation existed between a decision to retire early and the amount of expected pensions and annuity, including social security income after retirement. Other
economic factors were also important, though not para-
mount: asset level, preretirement savings, mortgage
payments and other debt obligation, and dependents.
Originally, one of the reasons that the UAW workers and
retirees were studied, was the presumption that both
preretirement and postretirement incomes within the UAW
group would be homogeneous, at least comparatively so. In
fact, the income levels in the group sampled were considerably more heterogeneous than expected and this situation provided further validation of the correlation between
the retirement decision and financial factors, since preretirement income level turned out to be very useful in differentiating between retirees and non-retirees.

The next most significant association between the early
retirement decision and a situational variable, or at least
what seemed to be a situational rather than an attitudinal
variable at that time, was with health status. Leaving aside
those whose health was so poor as to force retirement, even
in disabled status, those who assessed their health as poor or
declining were the most likely candidates for early retire-

ment. Other factors were less significant than expected. Except for those working in early retirement-intensive industries and those occupations where service length, not age, is the major consideration for retirement (for example, the military) occupation was not highly correlated with the decision to retire early. Neither were education, socioeconomic status, nor employment status of a spouse significantly associated with early retirement. More specific factors were investigated in the UAW study and it was demonstrated that neither a routine repetitive job, nor traveling time, nor relationships with co-workers were significantly related to the early retirement decision either. However, several other variables were associated positively with early retirement in the UAW group: hobbies, perceived and actual pressure from the union to retire early, a desire for less work, and some job dissatisfaction. Finally, a person who participated in a planning or discussion session about early retirement, apparently not yet committed to early retirement, appeared to become committed subsequent to the participation.

As early retirement benefits increased and more persons began to avail themselves of the opportunities presented to leave work, concern began to mount about the determinants of the decision. Two interesting points raised by Orbach's study, done about the same time as the original Barfield and Morgan two-tier study, provoked many questions.[16] First, people who retired early tended to save more than those who had not planned early retirement; and second, the majority of early retirees were not those who had made the decision but those who had been retired involuntarily. After early retirement benefits had been increased, three questions became more pressing, since the likelihood was greater than

16. Harold I. Orbach, *Trends in Early Retirement* (Ann Arbor, 1969), see especially pp. 14-33.

before that retirees had chosen to leave the labor force voluntarily.

— Do survivors' pensions with reduced benefits affect the early retirement decision?

— Does early retirement have a cycle coinciding with the American business cycle and how do these cycles interact?

— Is the positive trend toward early retirement a product of employer pressures and inducements to unplanned early retirement or is it chiefly due to purely economic gains in retirement income brought about by increased pension benefits?

In addition to these questions, the generally positive attitude toward early retirement which was apparent in virtually all publications on the issue, whether concerned about the decision, planning for early retirement, the early retirement experience, or the macroeconomic impact of continuing trends toward early retirement, was not echoed by all analysts. In 1970, Kreps made a significant statement about the costs of early retirement, and the appearance of that article heralded a reaction against the generally supportive view of early retirement so common until recently.[17]

Kreps sees early retirement as just one kind of response to technological change and the perceived necessity of altering the composition of the labor force consequent upon such change. However, the fact that retirement and early retirement will take place in a context of increased technological change presents problems that, in Krep's view, are as significant as those the early retirement option was supposed to alleviate. As she states: "The faster the pace of technology

---

17. Juanita Kreps, "Economics of Aging: Work and Income Through the Lifespan," *American Behavioral Scientist 14* 1 (1970), pp. 31-90.

and the higher the rate of economic growth, the greater is the disparity between earning and retirement benefits, under the present income allocation arrangements. Hence in a relative sense, economic deprivation of the nonworking aged is generated in the process of technological advance and growth." Barfield and Morgan, as well as others, suggest that the prospect of early retirement is positively associated with frugality and saving during working years, a thriftiness not so evident in the saving behavior of those who do not plan early retirement. Kreps suggests that this frugal behavior serves as a depressant to the economy both during and after the working years of these retirees. While they work, they save and do not consume as much as they would without such retirement-oriented saving. When they are retired, their incomes do not permit a high level of consumption. Even at such a moderate rate of inflation as 3 percent, a retiree depending upon 48 percent of his preretirement income after retirement (a generous estimate) will, after 20 years, see that proportion decline to 27 percent. Obviously early retirees with no health problems have an excellent chance to "enjoy" retirement for 20 years at least.

Poverty among older Americans may become as threatening a spectre to the aged in the late twentieth century as it was in the nineteenth century simply because retirement income for most will lag so far behind working income. There are only three major ways in which retirement income can be obtained and be secured: individual savings and assets; private pension arrangements; and transfer payments through taxation. Individual savings, at the present time, show no sign of increasing dramatically. Indeed, the consuming behavior of Americans over the past inflationary decade has eroded savings and built an enormous consumer debt. Private pension plans do not provide sufficient support in and of themselves. Moreover, it is important to recognize that, at present, the federal government supports private pension payments through the corporate tax structure. Finally, by the end of the century fewer than two workers will be supporting one beneficiary, by payroll tax, a situation which will undoubtedly result in benefits which may be much reduced in real value by inflation.

While larger economic issues have now been introduced into the early retirement research arena by Kreps, attention continues to focus upon the early retirement decision.

In a study of UAW workers and retirees done by Pollman and Johnson,[18] it was hypothesized that changes in jobs or the addition of extra tasks to a job might be positively associated with an early retirement decision. Consequently, there was interest in determining whether specific jobs were more likely to produce an early retirement decision, all other things being equal, than others. No relationship was found between specific job class and early retirement, but changes in performance on the job, changes in the job itself, and added tasks and responsibilities did have a positive association with an early retirement decision. This study gives a more specific understanding of the interaction between job satisfaction and the early retirement decision. Change, especially what might be perceived as negative and burdensome change, was the important element. Obviously, management has, within the spectrum of change permitted by work rules, the option to vary the amount of satisfaction thus influencing the early retirement decision.

These concerns and studies set the stage for a series of research efforts which examine the early retirement decision in more careful detail. A doctoral dissertation by Richard Burkhauser completed in 1976 developed a relatively sophisticated model for testing the role of economic

---

18. A.W. Pollman and A.C. Johnson, "Resistance to Change, Early Retirement and Managerial Decisions," *Industrial Gerontology 1* 1 (1974), pp. 33-41.

variables in pension acceptance.[19] Present value of the pension as well as variants with age of acceptance, the effects of pension constraints, the alternative value of the potential retiree's time, in addition to the health of the individual and the effect of assets other than pension were included in the model. The model appears to have predictive power, in that auto workers given the opportunity to decide to accept a pension behaved in the predicted manner. Both the difference in the asset value of the pension and the value of potential wages lost by acceptance were important. Health recedes as an all-important factor in this study, with the exception of those whose health forces retirement upon them. But both the healthy and those in ill-health responded to economic incentives. Those whose family assets were greater tended to accept pensions in greater numbers. Of those accepting pensions, meaning those who decided for early retirement from their employment, over 80 percent of those studied remained out of the labor force. Both education and family assets were important influences in decisions to remain outside the labor force. Clearly, this work demonstrates that workers are sensitive to pension benefits and economic incentives.

Yet another analysis of the retirement decision was a cross-sectional study by J.F. Quinn of white males in the Social Security Administration Retirement History study.[20] To some degree, this study was conducted to correct errors which may have arisen from flaws in previous surveys, including Barfield and Morgan's, while a second impetus developed from a concern about the conceptual basis of previous studies.

The Quinn findings about the early retirement decision both confirm and alter some earlier conclusions. Both health

---

19. Richard Burkhauser, "The Early Retirement Decision and Its Effect on Exit from the Labor Market," unpublished Ph.D. Dissertation, University of Chicago, 1976.

20. J.F. Quinn, "Microeconomic Determinants of Early Retirement: Cross-Sectional View of White Married Men," *Journal of Human Resources 12* 3 (1977), pp. 329-346.

and early retirement eligibility were found to be important determinants in the decisions and, equally important, there was found to be substantial interaction between these two major determinants. According to Quinn, the flow of asset income is significant and its significance is greater with individuals in poor health, just as those individuals are more likely to accept pensions and retire early. The income realized from pensions as well as other sources appears to be more closely correlated with decisions made by those in middle-income ranges than with decisions made by those at either the low or the high end of the range of incomes. Although this sensitivity is important within this income range, it declines at either end of their income spectrum for different sets of reasons. Quinn's study also assessed retirement probabilities with respect to situational and attitudinal variables studied by others. Retirement probabilities are lower in tight labor markets, compared to those sections of the country where the markets are less restricted. This finding suggests that earlier findings may not have correctly assessed how workers respond to tight markets at different times. In contrast to Pollman and Johnson's conclusions that early retirement was not significantly associated with undesirable work (an understandable conclusion in a study where the group observed, the UAW workers and retirees was relatively homogeneous), Quinn found that undesirability of a job did associate positively with the early retirement decision in this national sample and that this positive association was increased considerably in those who reported ill health. While noting that it is not possible to extrapolate such cross-sectional data, Quinn does suggest that some generalizations can be made over time and that these indicate that changes in public and private pension programs as well as the interactions between them do have significant labor force ramifications. Therefore, if there are macroeconomic concerns of the sort discussed by Kreps though largely ignored by workers in the early retirement research area, policymakers would be well-advised to restrain initiatives to lower the age eligibility for social security benefits on a wholesale basis. Extending disability would, in Quinn's view, meet some of the objectives early retirement is designed to achieve while suppressing the negative impact of large-scale withdrawal of able-bodied persons from the labor force at younger and younger ages. The Quinn study is valuable, not only for the critical view it takes of previous work, and for the high quality and careful presentation of its own findings, but for its demonstration of the complexity of the research problem at hand.

More recently, Barfield and Morgan returned to their UAW workers, moved in part by the questions raised by the first study, in part by the changes which have taken place in the economy over the past decade, and partly in response to concerns about planning retirement.[21] In a later section, attention will be devoted to the emerging retirement planning orthodoxy which is closely connected to the development of educational opportunity for older Americans. Apostles of this orthodoxy appear to imagine candidates for early retirement as persons well-acquainted with their postretirement prospects at least as far as finances are concerned. Barfield and Morgan found that such a large number of UAW members professed ignorance of the amount of retirement pension they could expect that it was impossible to use this measure in the data analysis. Historical experience turned out to be very important to the early retirement decision in this study. Not only does growing up in the Depression or living through a recession seem important, but the numerous ways in which people experienced these hard times appear crucial to retirement discussions. Although it is necessary to keep in mind that the Barfield and Morgan study sample is relatively homogeneous and that the results ought not to be

---

21. Richard Barfield and James Morgan, "Trends in Planned Early Retirement," *Gerontologist 18* 1 (1978), pp. 13-18.

magnified or extended, it was claimed that low income was significantly associated with early retirement, contrary to expectation. This low income reflects, for many, long term employment difficulties. Escape into early retirement, in uncomfortably straitened circumstances, may not differ appreciably from annual incomes reduced each year by periods of unemployment.

A further association, not with income or income level, appeared significant. Marital status mattered for UAW members. Single men were much more likely to retire early. Among married men, those who are comparatively young or who expect additional pension income from one source or another are more likely to report that they plan early retirement. Married women report such plans when there is a high family income, no mortgage payments, and no commitments to children that would be carried on to the postretirement years.

This study is, of course, more specific than the earlier UAW studies, and from it a more complex picture emerges of the possible early retiree. Given the relatively narrow spectrum of persons available in the UAW membership, those with low incomes, those with troubled work histories, and those with no responsibilities tend to retire or to plan on doing so. Those with resources besides pensions, for example income of other family members, and without significant financial responsibility also plan to retire early. But even within that latter group, it is clear that planning to retire and planning for retirement in a specific financial way are not the same thing.

In an unpublished study, Berman and Holtzman[22] studied yet another UAW group, this time the members of the local

22. Harry J. Berman and Joseph M. Holtzman, "Early Retirement Decisions: Factors Differentiating Retirees from Non-Retirees," paper presented at the 31st Annual Scientific Meeting of the Gerontological Society, Dallas, November 18, 1978.

at the Fiat-Allis Construction Machinery plant in Spring-
field, Illinois. In this case, on January 1, 1978, a new pension
plan went into effect which eliminated reduced payments for
early retirees. In addition, a formula for eligibility which
combined age and length of service was replaced by a provision based on years of service only. Of the 2,000 workers in
this plant, 324 individuals immediately became eligible for
early retirement when the contract became effective, and of
this number, 73, or 23 percent, of those eligible actually did
retire. All workers choosing early retirement would receive
the same amount—$650 per month—until they reached the
regular retirement age of 62. At that time, social security
benefits would take effect as well as the regular pension
payments based on grade and length of service.

In this research, the retirees were compared with a group
which had elected not to retire. Several interesting results
emerged from this set of interviews. On average, retirees
tended to be a little older than non-retirees, although the difference was not statistically significant. Retirees had fewer
years of formal education. Early retirees tended either to
own their own homes free and clear or to be renters more
than the non-retirees who tended to have mortgages. Retirees
reported that they had fewer retired friends than the non-
retirees although there was no difference between the two
groups in the extent to which they reported that their retired
friends either were or were not satisfied with retirement. This
study revealed no association between the early retirement
decision and marital status or number of children living at
home. Neither did any differences emerge between retirees
and non-retirees relating to financial status, including having
regular outside work, receiving additional income from
family members, or having the responsibility of making a
contribution to some family member's livelihood. Further,
there appeared to be no significant difference between the
two groups with respect to community involvement, volun-

tary associations, or friendships. It may be significant that one question did discriminate between the two groups. People who had decided not to retire perceived that they were better off than they had expected to be when they left school many years before, while those choosing to retire early thought that they were just about as well off as they had expected to be. It is difficult to conclude anything on so little evidence, but it is possible that a sense of achievement beyond expectation might prove to be an incentive to continue in a life pattern which had been satisfying.

A positive association was found between one indirect health indicator, the perceived necessity for limiting some activity because of health, and the early retirement decision. Leisure activities and participation in them did not differ from one group to the other. The financial status of those who chose early retirement was, on the average, a little lower than the average income of those who chose not to retire, an inverse relationship which the authors indicate is contrary to the early findings of Barfield and Morgan—although it agrees with the results of the second Barfield and Morgan study. Quinn's study indicates that a positive association between income, and assets as well, exists strongly only for middle income early retirees.

Understanding of the early retirement decision and its relationship to income across groups is limited because most information has come from a narrow range of blue-collar workers and studies based on large national samples have only just begun to investigate the relationship between income level and the early retirement decision among other income and occupational groups. Moreover, contextual variables such as the state of the economy at the time of the study may have significant influence upon such decisions which only large-scale longitudinal studies will reveal.

One objective of the Berman and Holtzman research was to validate and complete the typology of the voluntary early retiree—a typology including such elements as the ownership of a home free and clear, the completion of responsibility for children, relatively good health, considerable job satisfaction, extensive involvement in leisure and community activities, and possibilities of extending moonlighting to postretirement work if necessary or desirable. This idealized picture probably owes more to the wishful thinking characteristic of retirement planners than to what the literature, sparse as it is, really reveals. Moreover, it is possible that the conceptualization is also contaminated a little by the generally positive experiences associated with the groups who were at one time almost the only early retirees—military personnel who have for many years gained substantial pensions, as some civil servants do, based chiefly on grade and length of service rather than age. Such early retirees, investigated at some length by Biderman,[23] often undertake second careers with the financial security necessary to obtain retraining and assistance with job search. Both these early retirees and the idealized picture of early retirees differ from the less favorable picture of the typical early retirees at Fiat-Allis. Generally, the Fiat-Allis retirees were less advantaged than non-retirees. With fewer years of education, lower income, and more health problems, this group of retirees would be less likely to "enact the retirement role" successfully, in the words of Atchley,[24] than their non-retired associates. Moreover, the psychological measures used indicate that the early retirees had more negative affect, higher anomia, a relatively external locus of control, and a lesser degree of achievement of life expectations. High achievement of life expectations is a strong predictor of lifelong satisfaction in retirement.

23. Albert D. Biderman, "The Retired Military," in Roger W. Little, ed., *Handbook of Military Institutions* (Beverly Hills, CA, 1971), pp. 123-163.

24. Robert Atchley, *The Sociology of Retirement* (New York, 1976), pp. 18 ff.

Since it is not likely that new, broadbased studies dedicated exclusively to the determinants of early retirement in all the populations will be undertaken, it is appropriate to conclude this discussion with some reference to the analysis of early retirement provided by Parnes.[25] This longitudinal study of the labor market experience of men provides a body of data readily available in good condition to research workers who wish to perform secondary analyses. The conceptual framework used by Parnes for devising their design, collecting information, as well as analyzing and interpreting data, presents five sets of factors as influential in determining whether an individual will or will not choose early retirement. These factors are financial need, financial resources, ability to work, economic and noneconomic rewards of work, and relative preference for leisure over income. Few surprises can be found in these data. Clearly the availability of benefits was of great significance in the decision to retire early, and the author notes that his conclusions are, on balance, similar to those reached by Barfield and Morgan in the early study. Moreover, Parnes points out that there was an increase of 10 percentage points in intention to retire early within a group questioned in both 1966 and in 1971. Despite the emphasis on attitudinal factors, he ascribes most of this increase in intention to the increasingly liberalized benefits. Few early retirees show labor market activity after retirement, indicating, by indirect measures, preference for leisure over income and the perceived lack of noneconomic rewards for work. According to Parnes, attitudinal factors are important because this labor market inactivity does not vary with health status. It is important to note that this study stresses the impossibility of arriving at appropriate conclusions about reasons for retirement by relying exclusively on

---

25. Herbert S. Parnes *et al., The Pre-Retirement Years Volume 4. A Longitudinal Study of the Labor Market Experience of Men,* U.S. Department of Labor, Manpower Research and Development, Monograph No. 15 (Washington, 1975).

attitudinal measures, since there is a great deal of ambiguity in the meaning of a whole range of terms, including the meaning of ill health.

There are three groups of early retirees. The voluntary early retiree in the Parnes study is male, in his fifties, in relatively good health, with financial resources to meet his own needs and those of his dependents. The voluntary retiree can take full advantage of early retirement benefits and is prepared to enact the retirement role.

The involuntary early retiree can be one of several types. Obviously those who retire early because of ill health as well as those whose jobs are eliminated, the Packard workers Aiken, Ferman and Sheppard[26] studied, belong to this group. But more recent studies suggest that a third group of early retirees, not precisely involuntary yet not truly voluntary either, can be identified.[27] Some of the Fiat-Allis workers were clearly of this type, the unprepared early retiree. While it is true that the development and extension of the early retirement option has been a distinct advantage to voluntary and involuntary retirees, questions remain about how and why early retirement is chosen by persons in this third category of unprepared retirees. These questions are important because the factors which influence the early retirement decision have a major impact on the postretirement experience.

---

26. Aiken, Ferman, and Sheppard, *Economic Failure, Alienation, and Extremism,* pp. 43 ff.

27. Elizabeth G. Heidbreder, "Factors in Retirement Adjustment: White Collar/Blue Collar Experience," *Industrial Gerontology 12,* (Winter 1972), pp. 69-79.

Chapter 3
The Early Retirement
Experience: Individual Outcomes
and Social Consequences

The early retirement experience begins during the process of decisionmaking about labor force withdrawal. There are three categories of persons entering upon the experience: those for whom the decision was voluntary; those for whom retirement was involuntary whether for reasons of health or inability to obtain and retain employment; and another less obvious group of persons, those not actually forced to retire by ill health or unemployment who appear to choose early retirement as the least negative option open to them. Whether the retirement decision of this last group is completely voluntary or not, they appear to be less prepared for retirement than voluntary early retirees and in some senses resemble involuntary early retirees.

Approaches to Retirement Research

Research concerning the early retirement experience is based, whether explicitly or not, on the notion that intervention is one product of research. Thus far, there appear to be two intervention-oriented perspectives from which the retirement experience has been viewed.

One major approach to the study of the postretirement experience might be called the "unemployment-outcome" approach, which often assumes negative outcomes for all early retired populations, regardless of whether the early retirement is freely chosen or not. It generally expresses surprise when the negative outcomes do not appear on schedule. Another major approach relies little on the traditional genres of labor market research and stresses a life cycle perspective. Despite protestations to the contrary, this approach, heavily favored by planners and educators, tends to assume freely chosen early retirement, and reacts with astonishment at the intransigence of its data on lower-income involuntarily retired persons. However, before any suggestions can be made about a more appropriate synthesis designed to provide a conceptual basis for future study, it is necessary to draw together this research, to examine the validity of the conclusions reached, and to move beyond the constraints imposed by these implicit assumptions.

Let us first consider the "unemployment-outcome" style of early retirement research. The correlation of unemployment, in itself or as one factor in large-scale economic change, with negative physical and mental health consequences, has its foundations in Durkheim's study of suicide.[1] The proposed connection between macroeconomic events and individual experience has been investigated by economists, sociologists, and social psychologists for the past 80 years, but only recently has the correlation been firmly established by the works of Brenner, Catalano and Dooley, Cobb and Kasl.[2] Although many aspects of the correlation are still debated and while fundamental questions are still raised, the connections between unemployment and

1. Emile Durkheim, *Suicide,* translated by J.A. Spaulding and George Simpson (Glencoe, IL, 1951).

2. M.H. Brenner, *Mental Illness and the Economy* (Cambridge, 1973); see also Cobb and Kasl and Catalano and Dooley, in L.A. Ferman and J.P. Gordus, *Mental Health and the Economy* (Kalamazoo, 1979).

negative physical and mental health indicators have been so clearly demonstrated that what might be called an "unemployment-outcome" approach for retirement has either been explicitly adopted or implicitly assumed in numerous research studies on retirement. Since retirement, early or late, is a transition with enormous impact on all aspects of the retirees' lives, it is not surprising that observers have hypothesized that similar negative mental and physical health outcomes would follow upon retirement, especially retirements in which a certain amount of economic deprivation is encountered.

Retirement and Physical Health Outcomes

An intervention strategy normally associated with negative unemployment outcomes would stress programs which would provide phased and partial withdrawal from the labor force, assistance with retention or re-entry to the labor force, or some combination of the two.

The life-cycle approach to retirement research regards that latter portion of life in which leisure replaces work as a normal rhythm of life. There should be little that is disruptive about this change unless poor health or economic deprivation must be endured. Atchley maintains that the transition from work to retirement can be smooth, that self-respect may suffer if income drops drastically, but that "as retirement becomes more an expected part of the life-cycle, work may be seen as a temporary phase of life than the dominant life function for many people."[3] Interventions associated with this approach would emphasize planning for retirement and the availability of a wide range of leisure programs for retired persons. Educational programs, both for the planning as well as continuing education for leisure, are

3. Robert C. Atchley, "Retirement and Leisure Participation: Continuity of Crisis," *The Gerontologist 2* 1 (Spring 1971), p. 1.

developed to assist with the transition from work and to provide a type of work-substitute activity.

An early study designed to test the hypothesis that retirement itself is a stressful event likely to have deleterious consequences leading perhaps to death depended upon military data for Army and Air Force officers who retired between 1925 and 1948.[4] In this 1955 study, McMahan and Ford divided the group studied into cohorts according to age-at-retirement. These groups spanned the early-retirement spectrum and went beyond it; the groups were aged 50-54, 55-59, 60-64, and 65-69. The retirement period for each group was itself divided into three five-year segments. The rationale for this categorization was that the stressful aspects of retirement would be found in the first five years after retirement. However, in no age group were there any significant increases in mortality for the first five year period over any other five year period after retirement. This study has several interesting aspects. For the period in which it was done, it was an unprecedented study of early retirees, since military personnel were one of the few groups in American society to whom early retirement was not only possible but even mandatory depending upon rank. Moreover, retirement was expected. Even in those cases when retirement was mandatory after failure to achieve a certain rank, the retiree knew several years in advance when his retirement would take place. To some degree, these retirees were also provided with sufficient resources to live comfortably without work; they also, in many cases, had acquired skills in the military which, either with or without additional training, prepared them well for second careers.

Shortly after the military study, an investigation of the health status of retirees was undertaken by Tyhurst, Salk,

---

4. C.A. McMahan and T.R. Ford, "Surviving the First Five Years of Retirement," *Journal of Gerontology 10* 2 (1955), pp. 212-215.

and Kennedy.[5] This study involved employees in the communications industry, before, after and up to fifteen years beyond retirement. For many of these workers, retirement was at the usual age of 65, although some had retired earlier. The study was a combination of archival research in the health records of the employees and survey research with a series of questions about adjustment and health. Although some retirees in the sample of 257, about 25 percent, reported some difficulty adjusting to retirement, the majority of all retired persons in the sample reported good health status. Moreover, comparison with the health records indicated that subjective feelings of health improved after retirement.

Retirement and Mental Health Outcomes

A more specific mental health correlation study was conducted by Lowenthal and Berkman in San Francisco shortly after the Tyhurst, Salk, and Kennedy study.[6] Although this research was carried out in 1960-62, it was not published until 1967. The study does not specify early retirement, but its findings have indirect implications for early retirement. Retirement, it was found, is significantly associated with mental and emotional impairment if other "deprivational factors" are present. Such factors include low socioeconomic status, low level of social activity, and poor physical health. The measures of mental impairment used in this study included the subjective reactions of the interviewer, a rather complex and carefully constructed instrument designed to provide more objective measures, plus a number of tests designed to test cognition, short term memory, and long term memory. It was not an intention of

5. S.A. Tyhurst, J.E. Salk, and D.E. Kennedy, "Mortality, Morbidity, and Retirement," *American Journal of Public Health 47* 3 (1957), pp. 1434-1444.

6. M.I. Lowenthal and P.M. Berkman, *Aging and Mental Disorder in San Francisco* (San Francisco, 1967).

this research group to suggest that, in some cases, persons comparatively "deprived" were more likely to be retired, and therefore more likely to be present in their study sample. Consequently, the emphasis of this work is not the sequential association of retirement with decay, characteristic of the "unemployment-outcome" model. In fact this work challenges the utility of that model, albeit implicitly.

A major study extending over a substantial period in the late 1950s and early 1960s was reported by Streib and Schneider in 1971.[7] This was a large sample of about 2,000 persons, of whom about 500 (25 percent) were women. Unfortunately, no early retirees were included in this group. The duration of the study was such that interviews were done before, at the time of, and after retirement. A wide range of factors was considered in this study. The results of this research indicate that the physical and mental health of all cohorts in the study declined just a little, although comparisons between sample members still working and those who were retired and a little older did not reveal any significant differences. Moreover, when failing health was identified, the subjects did not attribute it to retirement, or more specifically to any perceived difficulties or objective circumstances clearly associated with retirement.

This selection of studies gives a very clear idea of how retirement had come to be regarded by the 1960s. Providing that there was adequate planning for retirement, retirement itself was not to be regarded as a stressful transition, or at least not significantly so. It appeared, therefore, that retirement could actually improve health and well-being, or at least improve the retiree's perception of his condition.

---

7. G.F. Streib and C.J. Schneider, *Retirement in American Society* (Ithaca, 1971).

Research in the Early Retirement Experience

The next important step in the study of retirement, and the first real study of early retirement then appeared.[8] Although Barfield and Morgan's work on the early retirement decision has been analyzed at length, the results of the other major portion of the work, on the retirement experience, should be discussed at length in the context of other works on the retirement experience. The populations studied were working and retired persons chosen in a national sample study combined with a study of working and retired UAW members. The proposition put forth at the outset was provocative and important. Barfield and Morgan argued that studying early retirees was important because they were in the vanguard—that early retirees in the late 1960s would resemble "regular" retirees a decade later. Barfield and Morgan suggested that at the time, 1966-68, most retired persons had a lower level of formal education than their younger co-workers. Moreover, many older retirees at that time had neither social security nor private pensions, and that consequently, they existed as retirees at a level of deprivation which would not be characteristic of retirees a decade or more later on, as the more educated, affluent, and pension-covered groups began to retire. For the national sample, there was a clear inverse relationship between age and postretirement income. Such a relationship undoubtedly reflects the fact that those with very high preretirement incomes decided to retire, although this is only measured indirectly in this survey, through surrogate measures such as occupational status and educational level. In both samples, there was little suggestion of straitened circumstances; most people in both samples, over 65 percent, claimed to enjoy about the same standard of living, while about 34 percent

---

8. Barfield and Morgan, *Early Retirement.*

claimed that their retirement standard was lower than their preretirement standard of living. It is significant also that persons who retired when they had planned to do so had higher postretirement incomes on average than those who reported that they had not planned. Moreover, those who planned retirement worked for money after retirement far more often than those who retired unexpectedly; this association is closely related to ill health reported by many of those who retired more or less unexpectedly.

To some degree, the findings validate the initial proposition that early retirees in the 1960s would resemble regular retirees a decade later. Two groups of persons in both studies had low incomes; those who were older and those who had retired later and unexpectedly. This grouping suggested strongly that earlier retirement, alleged to be associated with higher educational status and therefore indirectly preretirement income level, did indeed correlate with higher educational achievement and therefore indirectly with income. Clearly, declining health was an important part of the decision to retire and it continued to be an important factor limiting satisfaction with retirement. Of those studied, 75 percent of the respondents in both groups professed themselves satisfied with retirement, while the 25 percent who were less satisfied or dissatisfied indicated that health played an important part in their problems. Respondents did not attribute poor health to the loss of the work role.

The Barfield and Morgan early retirees can be viewed retrospectively as a fortunate group. Those who had not cited ill health as a reason for retirement and who did not experience it during the course of the study seem to be that ideal type of early retiree Berman and Holtzman were to envision a decade later.[9] One important point to remember is

---

9. Berman and Holtzman, "Early Retirement Decisions."

that, at this stage, most retirement provisions of the type which the UAW was advocating did not yet provide disincentives for re-entry into the labor force. In some sense, this was an elite group whose presence on the pension rolls was perceived as neither a threat to a labor force they might re-enter nor to the national retirement resources to which they would no longer contribute. Further, several years were to elapse before inflation would make such inroads upon retirement incomes and a few more would pass before this interconnection between rapid technological change, early retirement, and eroded pension payments would be brought to national prominence.

It was a combination of these factors that led Barfield and Morgan to return to their study group in the UAW after a decade.

About 75 percent of the retirees interviewed by Barfield and Morgan in 1968 reported that they were satisfied with retirement. In 1976, only 56 percent of the retirees indicated they were "satisfied" or "very satisfied."[10] Lack of satisfaction correlated with both health and economic problems. No positive correlation between early retirement itself and lack of satisfaction was found, but it is significant that a group who had retired as early as they were able to were less satisfied with retirement than those who were eligible but had waited. No clearcut reasons emerged about this finding, although it is quite possible that in this group Barfield and Morgan did isolate a group whose comparative lack of adjustment may have been related to the loss of the work role. However, it is also possible that some of the problems reported were not apparent at an earlier date but had been present and unacknowledged before early retirement and may in fact have contributed in some way to the decision to retire as early as possible. Moreover, one might question

---

10. Barfield and Morgan, "Planned Early Retirement."

whether some of those retirees had had incentives beyond the financial ones for retirement, whether blocked opportunity, some supervisory pressure, plus psychological vulnerability to suggestion might have prompted a decision which might otherwise have been delayed.

However, the later Barfield and Morgan work had been preceded by an important study by Peretti and Wilson which examined the psychological consequences, not of early retirement *per se,* but of voluntary and involuntary retirement between the ages of 67 and 70.[11] The survey was made, and extended by less formal, open-ended interviews, of two groups: voluntary and involuntary retirees. The groups were matched according to age, income, and years of retirement. All were selected to be in good health. Factors which were examined included emotional satisfaction and stability, self-image, sense of usefulness, and the extent and quality of interpersonal relationships. Over all the independent variables, the results were constant in that the voluntary retirees expressed more satisfaction, indicated more stability, revealed that they held better self-images, and felt more useful than the involuntary retirees, as might have been expected. Involuntary retirees reported less satisfaction with retirement and reported more emotional problems, and it was clear that periods of depression were much more common among the involuntary retirees. A major contribution by Peretti and Wilson was a research design which controlled for preretirement mental health factors. Previously, the onus was placed upon early retirement itself as either an indicator of poor health, even in the absence of direct evidence of correlation, or as a stressful work-role transition which either exacerbated existing physical or mental health problems or provoked new ones. In the light of this work, it is very risky to im-

---

11. P.O. Peretti and R.C. Wilson, "Voluntary and Involuntary Retirement and Their Effects on Emotional Satisfaction," *International Journal of Aging and Human Development 6* 2 (1975), pp. 131-138.

plicate early retirement in this process although unemployment, even called by other names, has for older workers the negative physical and mental health outcomes which have been firmly established.

It is instructive to compare this study'with a much later analysis by Haynes, McMichael, and Tyrsler of survival after early and normal retirement.[12] In this research, which is a retrospective study comparing the mortality rates of two cohorts of retired rubber workers, Group I were normal retirees of age 65 and Group II were early retirees, aged 62-64. The early retirees, Group II, exhibited increased mortality rates compared with a group of subjects who worked during that same age span. The higher mortality rate of early retirees appears to be correlated with health before retirement, specifically the last two years before retirement. The normal retirees did not show any increase in mortality rates. This finding suggests that preretirement health status, not retirement—either early or regular—is more significant for postretirement health status than the stress induced by the change from work to retirement.

Sociologists have not been alone in the demythologizing of retirement, early or late. While it is always difficult to associate findings from psychiatry or clinical psychology with broad sociological studies or the epidemiological kind of studies done by public health research groups, the psychiatric literature resounds with affirmation of some of the social science findings. An excellent example of literature review plus medical observation, so characteristic of the magisterial school of psychiatric writing, appeared in 1976. A.R. MacBride referred to retirement generally and did not reflect upon early retirement, but his conclusion, based on an exhaustive literature review, is simply that the common

12. S.G. Haynes, A.J. McMichael, and H.A. Tyrsler, "Survival After Early and Normal Retirement," *Journal of Gerontology 33* 2 (1978), pp. 269-278.

conception that retirement is a time of physical illness and psychosocial maladjustment is an assertion which has not borne up under the weight of investigational evidence, taken in various disciplines through a variety of techniques.[13] If that common misconception has a source, it is probably a combination of incorrect intuitions added to occasional striking case histories. Indeed, most good modern studies show the reverse; retirees benefit from retirement both physically and mentally, providing their health is adequate to begin with, their retirement is a chosen option, and that their resources are adequate for an acceptable style of life.

Debating Early Retirement Policies

Two articles, appearing in the same journal within a year, are now dated since they appeared nearly 15 years ago, yet they illustrate the two types of approaches to early retirement research and policy development mentioned earlier. Merton Bernstein, arguing against early retirement, adopts a labor force perspective and his points reflect that economic orientation.[14] Bernstein says that even when pensions are very good, they replace only about 50-60 percent of the working income, and early retirement options decrease that percentage still further. Moreover, he adds, retiring early decreases social security benefits and the entire arrangement adds costs for employers. Not all these arguments hold more than a decade later; many pension benefits have been arranged to equal "normal" benefits until social security begins and to decline thereafter. Further, it is certainly possible that early retirement can, in some instances, be profitable to management; it is surely not always a burden. However,

---

13. A.R. MacBride, "Retirement as Life Crisis: Myth or Reality," *Canadian Psychiatric Association Journal 21* 8 (1976), pp. 547-556.

14. M.C. Bernstein, "The Arguments Against Early Retirement," *Industrial Relations 4* 3 (1965), pp. 15-23.

Bernstein's arguments, although dated, take on validity because of the effects inflation has had upon what had seemed to be modest though adequate early retirement pension payments.

Bernstein also notes that pressures, rather than incentives, probably account for many early retirements and persons retire at the urging of management or unions to make place for younger entrants to the labor market although they would prefer to continue working. The reasons for wishing to remain on the job are not solely economic; a good deal of a person's social role is tied to his work role. Finally, Bernstein argues, it is not at all clear that this move toward early retirement will make more jobs available; if jobs once vacated close down without being filled by younger workers, this represents a net job loss. In the process, industry has lost an experienced worker.

Bernstein then presents a number of alternatives to early retirement including retraining programs and schemes for channeling resources now used for early retirement benefits into the promotion of job security. Finally he suggests, but does not elaborate upon, the scheme of partial-employment partial-retirement plans. This analysis and the recommendations following from it betray a certain lack of regard for management's ability to retain valued employees, to terminate less valuable workers, and to know the difference between the two. However, the underlying sentiment and rational is very clear; incentives should be offered and opportunities presented for persons to remain productive in the labor force. An incentive system should not be developed to drain workers out of the labor force since the welfare of individuals and the health of the economy are dependent upon continued employment, not increased early retirement.

A striking contrast with this view is found in Charles Odell's argument for early retirement.[15] In Odell's view, several factors account for the rise of early retirement. Improved benefits, disability benefits and special retirement provisions are the financial inducements he noted. Other factors loom very large, however; union programs for retired members on the national or international level, the development of older and retired workers' departments in unions, senior citizen centers, programs and activities sponsored by union locals, and retirement education programs are very important. To these, Odell added the provisions of the 1964 UAW agreements and the development of automation. From the perspective of a former union staff member specializing in programs for retired workers, the arguments for early retirement are less than half concerned with labor force problems, and a great deal of emphasis is laid, not upon the good things that retirement can bring workers, but on the function of social programming for a group of union members.

Both the Bernstein and Odell articles were first presented at an early retirement conference, and another article originating at that same conference presented by Melvin Bers survives the changes which have taken place during the intervening years much better.[16] Bers notes that unions had only recently begun to favor early retirement or mandatory retirement schemes and this change is related almost exclusively to the demographic shifts that have produced a tight labor market. In order to survive, unions must adapt and often that adaptation must take the form of pensioning off older workers, thus reducing factions and their power. At the time Bers wrote, early retirement was one of the few

15. Charles E. Odell, "The Case for Early Retirement," *Industrial Relations 4* 3 (1965), pp. 24-32.

16. Melvin K. Bers, "Equity and Strategy in Union Retirement Policy," *Industrial Relations 4* 3 (1965); see also Max D. Kossoris, "Early Retirement: An Overview," *Industrial Relations 4* 3 (1965), pp. 33-41.

issues upon which management and labor could agree, although for very different reasons. Not only does Bers' approach to a national employment problem differ in emphasis from most of the other early studies of early retirement, but the absence of an underlying intervention strategy sets it apart from those studies which are oriented toward the social or planning side of retirement studies.

Planning and Programming for Early Retirement

Even Barfield and Morgan had indicated in their second UAW analysis that they had thought that planning might be important.[17] Their first important finding in that resurvey was that their respondents had a very poor notion of what income they would have after retirement, even when that retirement was imminent. The term "planning" in the retirement literature is ambiguous. Sometimes, as in Barfield and Morgan, it means what the individual considering retirement has in mind for the future, how the available resources are accounted, and how it is expected that changes in lifestyle will be made most conveniently. Planning also can mean those services offered to the person intending to retire or eligible for early retirement by a whole host of agencies, unions, community groups, and local institutions.

Each of these major sectors has a special interest in older Americans. Obviously, labor unions have concluded arrangements with management for early retirement benefits for older workers, and have adopted a strategy that dictates encouragement of early retirement among union members for the sake of the union itself. Therefore labor unions have a special interest in providing planning services and special sessions which could, and the literature indicates certainly do, facilitate a decision to retire early among previously uncommitted participants.[18] In periods where economic growth

---

17. Barfield and Morgan, "Planned Early Retirement."
18. e.g., Barfield and Morgan, Early Retirement.

is slow, unions will continue to emphasize the benefit side of the wage-benefit package and benefits are often an important target for reduction demands on the part of management in the next round of bargaining. In fact, in at least one instance, a major union which secured a benefit for its members mounted a major campaign to inform members about the benefit and to urge its use so that it would not be subject to criticism and withdrawal for lack of use.[19]

In an earlier section, mention was made of the Older Americans Act of 1965. The implementation of this legislation at the local level has created a kaleidoscopic set of programs and centers for senior citizens and retired persons. Some are free-standing while others either provide or are subject to coordinating efforts among municipal, county, and state organizations. Moreover, funds flow from several federal sources and a wide range of local authorities as well. For reporting purposes, careful counts are made of persons availing themselves of the services offered by these groups. Continual growth is important for the maintenance of many programs. These programs are geared, by statute or by constituency, to the needs and interests of older persons, most often post-65 retirees, or even 70 year olds, providing assistance with health and legal issues, recreation, education, and travel opportunities. In these programs, practitioners observe on a daily basis the problems encountered by older Americans who have not, for one reason or another, been able to plan for their retirement. In response, such agencies often reach out to the preretirement population so as to serve better their clientele by serving them earlier.

Educational institutions have become particularly active in the area of gerontology. In order to use buildings which have been or are being emptied by the decline of the birth rate,

---

19. Use by the outpatient psychiatric care benefit was stimulated by arrangements made with community mental health centers. Letter from Judson Stone, Director, Six Area Coalition. Private communication, Sylvester Coleman.

school districts have come to emphasize adult education and continuing education activities. It is not unusual to see a local office of the HEW ACTION program, the Retired Senior Volunteer Program (RSVP), situated in a building which had been an elementary school. If elementary schools can provide alternative uses for their buildings, secondary schools can provide a whole range of courses. Very often such courses are available for a nominal fee or even free of charge for persons who are 55 and retired or 60, retired or not. The linkages have become even more numerous in many jurisdictions between local community colleges and senior groups as well as individuals. Once again, many states provide to the institutions a tuition waiver for older retired students, and community colleges that depend upon a declining pool of traditional-age applicants for their student body and whose enrollments are therefore declining reach out to this senior population. For example, subsidized meal programs for senior citizens also have a programmatic element and senior citizens who go to a center daily for a meal are, in some sense, a captive population for instruction. Many postsecondary educational institutions mount large programs in community centers, senior clubs, and even retirement housing. Most of these institutions also develop preretirement planning programs and courses which serve the dual purpose of providing service to older Americans while bolstering declining enrollments by recruiting new students. There can be little doubt that many of the services provided by these institutions are of value to retirees and their communities, but it would be idle to pretend that increasing numbers of retirees are not essential to the preservation and growth of these new or transfered service systems.

Life-Cycle Early Retirement Research: Planning and Program Development

An early study done at the University of Oregon in 1969 was composed of two mail surveys, one to companies inquiring about their early retirement benefits and policies and another covering individuals who had retired early.[20] There are some methodological difficulties with this study, but the results point toward benevolent company policies and satisfied retirees, persons who presumably had planned to retire and who had found the reality of retirement not very different from their envisioned life of leisure. All the studies done in the late 1960s have in common the fact that the early retirees studied had not been retired long and that inflation was not so serious a problem as it was to become. However, only five years after the Oregon study, Vincent Manion, who had been involved in that early work discussing issues and trends in preretirement education, noted that retirement early or late appears to involve many difficulties and that our current methods of dealing with these problems exacerbate them.[21] Preretirement education is virtually nonexistent, Manion asserted, and educational opportunities for coping with life after work should be offered long before the age of retirement. To some degree, present education available to retirees makes retirement seem very negative, for these courses and special sessions are addressed exclusively to the problem-solving part of retirement life. The negative ought not to be stressed either in content or curriculum. A suggestion is made by Manion that management should take responsibility for some retirement preparation for employees by paying tuition for positive preretirement educational opportunities.

---

20. Mark Greene, Charles Pyron, U. Vincent Manion, and Howard Vinklevoss, *Early Retirement: A Survey of Company Policies* (Eugene, OR, 1969).

21. U. Vincent Manion, "Issues and Trends in Pre-retirement Education," *Industrial Gerontology* (Fall 1974), pp. 13-21.

Another study by Malcolm Morrison also stresses the responsibility the private sector has for preparing employees for retirement and reports on a survey of blue-collar workers indicating that most of the respondents lacked the financial training and understanding to make an intelligent plan for retiring.[22] Moreover, and here Morrison agrees with the 1978 Barfield and Morgan findings, most of the respondents have a very unrealistic idea of what their retirement incomes and financial requirements will be. Since Morrison states that the respondents were of a "higher socioeconomic background than average," the clear implication of the findings is that a good fraction of those who were involuntarily retired and who chose early retirement as a less unattractive alternative to remaining in a job that had become burdensome are in no position to avail themselves of preretirement educational or planning services because they have so little ability to single out those conditions in the retirement decision and the retirement experience which may be crucial for them.

When initiatives toward early retirement were just beginning, when expansion seemed a constant condition of the American economy, these two intervention strategies, benevolent reduction of the labor force and a planned, secure, and active retirement life seemed closely connected, perhaps even ordained. The approaches for investigating early retirement seemed to fit together as well as anyone could reasonably expect when one formulation dealt with the economic determinants of reducing the labor force and providing subsidized early retirement while the other formulation depended upon how external changes in life states could conform to the stages of identity changes in individuals. It is true that the more economically-oriented style could easily be transformed into a variant of a sociological unemployment-outcome approach; however, the earliest

---

22. Malcolm H. Morrison, "The Myth of Employee Planning for Retirement," *Industrial Gerontology* (Spring 1974), pp. 23-31.

studies appeared to produce data which indicated that negative physical, psychological, and social outcomes were not connected with retirement as much as they were with unemployment. These data, of course, were drawn at an early stage from a relatively favored group whose benefits had not yet been eroded by inflation and whose early retirement was, after all, a subject of interest, investigation, and major collective bargaining initiatives.

If the unemployment-outcome approach was, to some degree, invalidated by biased data which contradicted its premises, the life-cycle approach which favored a smooth satisfactory transition from one life state to another subsequent to appropriate preparation also ran into difficulties. In one sense, Barfield and Morgan turned toward such an approach in their second analysis only to find that those data were more consistent with an unemployment-outcome approach.

Summary

Clearly the convenient congruity between labor force pressures and private fulfillment which had seemed so apparent as early retirement options were being developed and which seemed to bring together two different kinds of research agendas in so promising a fashion did not survive for long. In the early phase of research on early retirement, emphasis was placed upon the possibility that the transition from work to retirement might be stressful, even if postretirement income was adequate, just as unemployment is stressful. Those who studied early retirees in good health with adequate resources found that satisfaction levels were high and that the transition was smooth for many early retirees. The view that retirement is another phase of life, and that this phase should be fulfilling if preceded by preparation and planning, seemed most appropriate.

However, little if any of this research on the early retirement experience took place when inflation was annually reducing the purchasing power of pensions. While early research results might indicate that early retirement is not especially stressful, early retirement in a continued inflationary economy may very well become a negative experience.

Barfield and Morgan's first study was undertaken with the belief that the better-educated, more affluent early retiree of the 1960s would be typical of retirees generally a decade or two later. However, inflation has already reduced the affluence of those early retirees of the 1960s. Under these conditions, the retirement experience of Barfield and Morgan's regular retirees may, ironically, be more relevant than they had expected. Early retirement may become a stressful experience because of inflation and the interventions required would include retraining and job-search assistance consistent with the unemployment approach.

Chapter 4
The Future of Early Retirement:
Research Agendas and Policy Issues

Aging, work and retirement in American society have already been considered in one perspective. But despite the value of such a longitudinal view, especially as it demonstrates how and why some perceptions and practices arose, it is equally important to view aging, work and retirement as they are encapsulated in a social perspective.

The Social Dimensions of Aging and Retirement

There are certain social correlates to aging in any society, but several of them take on added importance at present.[1] Just as American society exhibits stratification along social lines, so there is stratification along age lines. Age stratification results in age inequalities, age segregation and age conflict.

---

1. What follows is a relatively standard analysis which follows closely the ideas in the Russell Sage Foundation volumes *Aging and Society:* Matilda White Riley and Anne Foner, *An Inventory of Research Findings,* Vol. 1 (1968); Matilda White Riley, John W. Riley, Jr., and Marilyn Johnson, *II Aging and the Professions,* Vol. 2 (1969); Matilda White Riley, Marilyn Johnson, and Anne Foner, *A Sociology of Age Stratification,* Vol. 3 (1972). See also, Matilda White Riley, "Age Strata in Social Systems" in Robert H. Blinstock and Ethel Shanas, eds., *Handbook of Aging and the Social Sciences* (1976).

For some age groups, mainly the young and the old, there is less access to roles which are valued by the society at large and restricted access to the rewards attached to those roles as well as other kinds of rewards. Work and the status and rewards associated with a work role are currently restricted to persons generally between 18 and 65 years of age, and the upper age limit at which a person can continue to have access to a valued and rewarded work role is being decreased by the gradual development of early retirement. Obviously the inequalities conferred by membership in the group into which a person is placed by age, irrespective of other qualifications, is a source of potential problems and conflict. Economic deprivation as a result of retirement which is more or less enforced at an earlier and earlier age is accompanied by other losses including social esteem and associated loss of self-esteem.

Age is also a criterion used to segregate one age group from another. The process of segregation by age begins almost at birth, but it is fortified by age-graded schools. To some degree, such segregation persists throughout the working years, but upon retirement the special burdens of age-segregation reinforced by age inequalities become heavier. Despite the benevolent impulses which dictate a whole range of services to older Americans, the programs developed often intensify the problems already associated with age segregation.

A combination of age inequality and age segregation, strengthened by the natural cohesion of cohorts—people born at the same time sharing the same historical context in a special way denied to those born at other times—permits, indeed almost dictates, the development of age conflict between different age groups. The intergenerational tensions that were so striking in eighteenth century America arose when older persons denied to younger persons wealth and power, often restricting access for younger persons to income and esteem associated with work roles and opportunities to move to the top in specific occupations. Currently, intergenerational tensions can reinforce the notion that persons older than 55, for example, are unproductive and should, by virtue of age, have restricted access to the income and valued social roles associated with work. However, another potential source of intergenerational tension is just now being recognized: the resentment that working members of society will feel toward those who draw from—or soon will draw from—the nation's retirement resources but who have not for quite some time, due to early retirement, contributed to those resources. Clearly an increasing trend toward early retirement can only exacerbate existing intergenerational tensions with the inevitable result that age inequality and age segregation will not only continue but intensify.

In the course of life, individuals move through a series of age-structured roles, and at the times when transitions are being made, individuals are especially vulnerable to stress. Not only does the actual change to new status cause strain, but there is often grief associated with the relinquishing of an old role which intensifies the stress encountered. When an individual adapts to a new role which is more highly valued, the stress is minimized. However, retirement for most in American society means stepping from a more valued to a less valued role.

The Costs and Benefits of Early Retirement

Early retirement, even for those who have planned their postretirement lives, who have adequate financial resources, and who are in relatively good health, has costs for early retirees themselves. Early retirees move from a role which usually has high status to one with lower status, and in the process they undergo the natural stress associated with any life change. In addition, early retirees could, in the future, become targets for resentment. If early retirees have their real purchasing power considerably eroded by inflation, or even if their purchasing power is lower than their expectations, then the intangible social and psychological costs of early retirement will become much more difficult for them to bear.

Early retirement can also have serious costs to individual companies and to the skill level of the labor market generally. If incentives to retire early are sufficiently attractive, many of those who choose to retire early will be those whose skills are valuable. Even a temporary shortage of skilled workers is costly. While there may be psychological and social costs to the early retirees themselves if their pensions are continually reduced in real purchasing power, increasing pension payments, if pensions have cost-of-living escalator clauses, will place more financial demands upon employers.

Finally, a continuing trend toward early retirement appears to have serious consequences for the national economy, straining retirement resources and generating tensions between age groups.

Early retirement also has benefits, both real and perceived. Many people retire early simply because they can and they wish to have leisure time. Departure from the labor force under ideal conditions does not threaten life or health and may actually prolong life and promote health. Early retirement can also be a response to ill health or negative employment experiences and prospects.

In order to develop policy alternatives in current early retirement practice, more information is essential on both costs and benefits of early retirement.[2] There is a need for

2. Harold R. Sheppard, *Employment Related Problems of Older Workers: A Research Strategy,* U.S. Department of Labor, R & D Monograph *73* (1979), presents a detailed outline of research priorities.

more research in the private and public pension plans having early retirement provisions to ascertain how many workers are covered and how many of those covered actually choose to retire early. Additional information about the actual financial condition of early retirees over time is necessary as well. Since economic deprivation may result from inflation eroding the benefits which are not indexed, and since social and psychological problems arise in response to economic deprivation, it is necessary to know how early retirees fare over a period of time. Although there is some suggestion that inflation may play a role in a decision to defer early retirement, the relationship between inflation and the early retirement decision requires investigation. Finally, research on the success of postretirement job search of early retirees is necessary.

Conventional wisdom in management may have suggested early retirement as a solution to older unproductive workers in the past, but the actual organizational results of continuing early retirement across a wide range of organizations are not known. Does the early retirement of an older worker whose pension is indexed actually represent the savings originally expected from this solution? Or is it possible that many early retired workers are living much longer and drawing pensions long beyond the anticipated and calculated period? Are those younger workers actually replacing older workers? Are they actually more productive?

Future Research and Policy Directions

The current state of knowledge of the impact of early retirement on individuals and the economy is limited, but it suggests the lines along which policy-related investigation should move.

One research perspective, the unemployment-oriented approach, has provided information which suggests that early retirement under the most favorable circumstances can be a smooth transition, but it also highlights the degree to which early retirement is a disguise for long term unemployment. The other research perspective, the life-cycle approach, emphasizes planning and preparation for early retirement as a critical variable in individual satisfaction with the retirement experience. These two approaches converge at several important junctures and emphasize those areas in which policy-related research questions must now be answered.

If early retirement is, for involuntary early retirees, a disguise for disability-related retirement for those in poor health and a disguise for terminal unemployment for those with troubled work histories, what would be the consequences of devising arrangements for disability pensions for the one group and retraining or public service employment for the unemployed? Such questions should be investigated on the individual level as well as the macroeconomic level. If early retirement is, for some early retirees, a choice of the lesser evil, a result of dissatisfaction with work and the employer's dissatisfaction with the worker, what would be the consequences of alternatives in the work place? What are the possibilities for restructuring jobs, lateral transfers, or phased retirements? Future studies should also be directed toward problems involved in the planning and implementation of such alternatives.

Early retirement has been a limited benefit to individuals, management, and labor, but it is a benefit which has an increasingly large cost. The history of early retirement shows two clear trends, one which increases incentives to retire early and the other which decreases incentives to remain in the labor force. Future policy should be developed in both directions, but the emphasis should be placed upon the productive retention of older workers. The focus for research and policy development must be shifted from early retirement to the larger area of work and aging.

SELECTED BIBLIOGRAPHY

Aaron, Henry J. "Demographic Effects on the Equity of Social Security Benefits," *The Economics of Public Services,* in Martin Feldstein and Robert Inman, eds. (London, 1977) pp. 151-173.

Achenbaum, W. Andrew. *Old Age in the New Land* (New York, 1978).

Aiken, Michael, Ferman, Louis A., and Sheppard, H.L. *Economic Failure, Alienation, and Extremism* (Ann Arbor, 1968) pp. 31-50.

Altmeyer, Arthur J. *The Formative Years of Social Security* (Madison, 1966).

Ando, Albert and Modigliani, Franco. "The Life-Cycle Hypothesis of Saving: Aggregate Implications and Tests," *American Economic Review 53* (1963) pp. 55-84.

Atchley, Robert. "Selected Social and Psychological Differences Between Men and Women in Later Life," *Journal of Gerontology 31* (1976) pp. 204-211.

Atchley, R. *The Sociology of Retirement* (New York, 1976).

Atchley, R. and Corbett, S. "Older Women and Jobs," in L.E. Troll and K. Israel, eds., *Looking Ahead* (Englewood Cliffs, 1977).

Bach, G.L. and Stephenson, James B. "Inflation and the Redistribution of Wealth," *Review of Economic Statistics 55* 1 (1974) pp. 1-13.

Bancroft, Gertrude and Garfinkle, Stuart. "Job Mobility in 1961," *Monthly Labor Review* (August 1963) pp. 897-906.

Barfield, Richard and Morgan, James. *Early Retirement: The Decision and the Experience* (Ann Arbor, 1969).

Barfield, Richard and Morgan, James. "Trends in Planned Early Retirement," *Gerontologist 18* 1 (1978) pp. 13-18.

Barsby, Steve L. and Cox, Dennis R. *Interstate Migration of the Elderly: An Economic Analysis* (Lexington, 1975).

Becker, Gary S. "A Theory of Social Interaction," *Journal of Political Economy 82* (1974) pp. 1064-1094.

Becker, Gary S. *Human Capital: A Theoretical and Empirical Analysis* (New York, 1964).

Bell, Donald R. "Prevalence of Private Retirement Plans," *Monthly Labor Review 98* 10 (1975) pp. 17-20.

Ben-Porath, Yoram. "Lifetime Income and Economic Growth—Comment," *American Economic Review 56* (1966) pp. 869-872.

Bergling, H. "Early Retirement Pensions in Sweden—Trends and Regional Variations," *Scandinavian Journal of Social Medicine 66* 1 (1978) pp. 7-16.

Berman, Harry J. and Holtzman, Joseph M. "Early Retirement Decisions: Factors Differentiating Retirees from Non-Retirees," paper presented at the 31st Annual Scientific Meeting of the Gerontological Society, Dallas, November 18, 1978.

Bernstein, Merton C. "The Arguments Against Early Retirement," *Industrial Relations 4* 3 (1965) pp. 29-38.

Bers, Melvin K. "Equity and Strategy in Union Retirement Policy," *Industrial Relations 4* 3 (1965); see also Kossoris, Max D., "Early Retirement: An Overview," *Industrial Relations 4* 3 (1965) pp. 33-41.

Birren, James E. "Age Changes in Skill and Learning," in *Earning Opportunities for Older Workers,* Wilma Donahue, ed. (Ann Arbor, 1955) pp. 67-74.

Bixby, Lenore. "Notes on Early Retirement: Program and Certain Personal Factors," U.S. Department of Health, Education and Welfare, Social Security Administration, Office of Research and Statistics, Research and Statistics Note No. 9, June 30, 1970.

Black, D.G. "Mandatory Retirement Law—Past and Future," *Baylor Law Review 30* 2 (1978) pp. 333-342.

Bolnick, Howard J. "The Regulation of Multiple Employer Trusts," *Best's Review (Life/Health) 78* 12 (1978) pp. 74-80.

Bond, K. "Retirement History Study's First Four Years: Work, Health and Living Arrangements," *Social Security Bulletin 39* 12 (1976) pp. 3-14.

Boskin, Michael J. "Economics of Labor Supply," in *Income Maintenance and Labor Supply,* Glen G. Cain and Harold Watts, eds. (New York, 1973) pp. 163-181.

Boskin, Michael J. "Social Security and Retirement Decision," *Economic Inquiry 15* 1 (1977) pp. 1-25.

Botwinick, Jack. *Aging and Behavior* (New York, 1973).

Bowen, William and Finegan, Thomas. *The Economics of Labor Force Participation* (Princeton, 1969).

Brackman, Theodore P. "Trust-Departments Face Employee Benefit Dilemma," *Trusts and Estates 115* 10 (1976) pp. 677-678, 690.

Brady, Dorothy S. "Influence on Age of Saving and Spending Patterns," *Monthly Labor Review 78* 11 (1955) pp. 1240-1244.

Brenner, M.H. *Mental Illness and the Economy* (Cambridge, 1973); see also Cobb and Kasl and Catalano and Dooley, in Ferman, L.A. and Gordus, J.P., eds., *Mental Health and the Economy* (Kalamazoo, 1979).

Brennan, Michael J., Taft, Philip, and Schupack, Mark B. *The Economics of Age* (New York, 1967).

Brimmer, Andrew F. "Inflation and Income Distribution in the United States," *Review of Economic Statistics 53* 1 (1971) pp. 37-48.

Brittain, John A. "The Incidence of Social Security Payroll Taxes," *American Economic Review 61* 1 (1971) pp. 110-125.

Brittain, John A. "The Incidence of the Social Security Payroll Tax: Reply," *American Economic Review 62* 4 (1972) pp. 739-742.

Brittain, John A. *The Payroll Tax for Social Security* (Washington, 1972).

Browning, Edgar K. "Social Insurance and Intergenerational Transfers," *Journal of Law and Economics 16* 2 (1973) pp. 215-237.

Browning, Edgar, K. "Labor Supply Distortions of Social Security," *Southern Economic Journal 42* 2 (1975) pp. 243-252.

Browning, Edgar K. "Why the Social Insurance Budget is Too Large in a Democracy," *Economic Inquiry 13* 3 (1975) pp. 373-388.

Bruff, N.H. "Presidential Exemption from Mandatory Retirement of Members of Independent and Regulatory Commissions," *Duke Law Journal 1976,* 2 pp. 249-279.

Buchanan, James M. "Social Insurance in a Growing Economy: A Proposal for Radical Reform," *National Tax Journal 21* (1968) pp. 386-395.

Burke, Burress Hayne. "Economic Crises for Women: Aging and Retirement Years," Fontbonne College (St. Louis) Series: MSS 1977 0726.

Burkhauser, Richard. "The Early Pension Decision and Its Effect on Exit from the Labor Market," unpublished Ph.D. dissertation, University of Chicago (1976).

Cagan, Phillip. *The Effect of Pension Plans on Aggregate Savings* (New York, 1965).

Cain, L.D. "Mandatory Retirement—Murgia Decisions and Likely Consequences," *Industrial Gerontology 3* 4 (1976) pp. 232-250.

Chen, Yung-Ping and Chy, Kwang-Wen. "Tax-Benefit Ratios and Rates of Return Under OASI: 1974 Retirees and Entrants," *Journal of Risk Insurance 41* 2 (1974) pp. 189-206.

Chu, K.W. and Solberg, E. "Early Retirement Vs. Labor-Force Participation of Aged—Impact on Social-Security Financing," *Gerontologist 17* 5 (1977) p. 47.

Clark, Lincoln H. *The Life Cycle and Consumer Behavior* (New York, 1955).

Clark, Margaret. "Cultural Values and Dependency in Later Life," in Cowgill, Donald and Holmes, Lowell, eds., *Aging and Modernization* (New York, 1972); Ross, Jennie-Keith, *Old People, New Lives: Community Creation in a Retirement Residence* (Chicago, 1977).

Clark, Robert. "The Influence of Low Fertility Rates and Retirement Policy on Dependency Costs," prepared for The American Institutes for Research in Behavioral Sciences, Washington, 1976.

Clark, Robert. "Increasing Income Transfers to the Elderly Implied by Zero Population Growth," *Review of Sociological Economics 35* 1 (1977) pp. 37-54.

Clay, Hilary M. "A Study of Performance on Relation to Age at Two Printing Works," *Journal of Gerontology 11* 4 (1956) pp. 417-424.

"Climbing Down the Ladder," *Management Review 67* 6 (1978) pp. 6-7.

Colamosca, A. " 'Grey Rights' Retirement Fight," *Dun's Review 110* 4 (1977) pp. 82-84.

Cook, Sherburne. "Aging of and in Populations," in P.S. Timiras, ed., *Developmental Physiology and Aging* (New York, 1972) p. 595.

Constandse, William J. "A Neglected Personnel Problem," *Personnel Journal 51* 2 (1972) pp. 129-133.

"Controversy Over Mandatory Retirement Age—Forward," *Congressional Digest 56* 11 (1977) p. 258. (sic)

Cowgill, D. "The Aging of Population and Societies," *Annals of the American Academy of Political and Social Science 415* (1974) p. 7.

Coyle, J. and Fuller, M. "Women's Work and Retirement Attitudes," paper presented at Annual Meeting of the Gerontological Society, San Francisco, 1977.

DeVanzo, Julie, De Tray, Dennis, and Greenberg, David H. "The Sensitivity of Male Labor Supply Estimates to Choice of Assumptions," *Review of Economic Statistics 58* 3 (1976) pp. 313-325.

David, Greg. "Employee Benefit Trusts' Growth Alarms Officials—More Failures Feared," *Business Insurance 11* 4 (1977) pp. 1, 32.

David, Greg. "Regulators Deplore Inaction by Labor on ERISA Trusts," *Business Insurance 11* 5 (1977) pp. 1, 68.

Davis, Harry E. "Multiemployer Pension Plan Provisions in 1973," *Monthly Labor Review* (October 1974) pp. 10-16.

Davis, Harry E. "Pension Provisions Affecting the Employment of Older Workers," *Monthly Labor Review 95* (1973) pp. 41-45.

Dernburg, Thomas and Strand, Kenneth. "Hidden Unemployment, 1953-62: A Qualitative Analysis by Age and Sex," *American Economic Review 56* (1966) pp. 71-95.

Donahue, T.B. "Early Retirement," *Harvard Business Review 53* 6 (1975) p. 172.

Donahue, Wilma T., ed., *Earning Opportunities for Older Workers* (Ann Arbor, 1955).

Dorfman, Robert. "The Labor Force Status of Persons Aged Sixty-Five and Over," *American Economic Review 44* (1954) pp. 634-644.

Drucker, G. "Mandatory Retirement and ADEA," *Industrial Gerontology 4* 4 (1977) pp. 272-276.

Durkheim, Emile. *Suicide,* eds. J.A. Spaulding and George Simpson (Glencoe, 1951).

Ekerdt, D. *et al.* "Longitudinal Change in Preferred Age of Retirement," paper presented at the Annual Meeting of the Gerontological Society, Lousiville, October 1975.

Elbaor, David W. "The Justice Department's First Move Under ERISA," *Journal of Pension Planning and Compliance 4* 1 (1978) pp. 63-69.

Epstein, Lenore A. "Early Retirement and Work-Life Experience," *Social Security Bulletin* (March 1966) p. 3.

Epstein, Lenore A. and Murray, Janet H. *The Aged Population of the United States: 1963 Social Security Survey of the Aged,* Office of Research and Statistics, SSA, Research Report No. 19, (Washington, 1967).

Epstein, *op. cit.,* p. 169.

Ibid., pp. 170-172.

Evans, D.F. "Changing from a What to a Who," *Business Horizons 20* 6 (1977) pp. 14-17.

Federal Reserve Bank of Boston. *Funding Pensions: Issues and Implications for Financial Markets,* Conference Series, No. 16 (Boston 1976).

Fischer, David Hackett. *Growing Old in America* (Oxford, England, 1978).

Flygare, T.J. "Mandatory Retirement is Fading Fast—Will Tenure be Next? *Phi Delta Kappan 59* 10 (1978) pp. 711-712.

Foley, A.R. "Preretirement Planning in a Changing Society," *American Journal of Psychiatry 128* 7 (1972) pp. 377-381.

Ford, L.C. "The Battle Over Mandatory Retirement," *Educational Record 59* 3 (1978) pp. 204-228.

Fox, J. "Effects of Retirement and Former Work Life on Women's Adaptation in Old Age," *Journal of Gerontology 32,* (1977) pp. 196-202.

Freeman, S. "Wage Trends as Performance Displays Productive Potential—Model and Application to Academic Early Retirement," *Bell Journal of Economics 8* 2 (1977) pp. 419-443.

Friedman, E. and Havighurst, R. *The Meaning of Work and Retirement* (Chicago, 1954).

Furseth, Byron J. "Retroactive Cure of Employee Plan Defects: When, What, and How," *Journal of Taxation 48* 4 (1978) pp. 220-223.

Gagliardo, Dominic. *American Social Insurance* (New York, 1955).

"Getting Rid of 65-and-Out," *Business Week* No. 2421 (1976) pp. 60-61.

Ghez, Gilbert and Becker, Gary. *The Allocation of Time and Goods Over the Life Cycle* (New York, 1975).

Givens, H. "Evaluation of Mandatory Retirement," *Annals of the American Academy of Political and Social Science 438* (1978) pp. 50-58.

Glamser, F. "Determinants of a Positive Attitude Toward Retirement," *Journal of Gerontology 31* (1976) pp. 104-107.

"Goals Important in Designing Savings, P-S Plans," *Employee Benefit Plan Review 33* 2 (1978) pp. 37-38.

Gorelik, M. "Mandatory Retirement," *AAUP Bulletin-American Association of University Professors 59* 3 (1973) p. 383.

Greene, Mark, Pyron, Charles, Manion, U. Vincent, and Vinklevoss, Howard. *Early Retirement: A Survey of Company Policies* (Eugene, Oregon, 1969).

Grossman, Michael. "On the Concept of Health," *Journal of Political Economy 80* (1972) pp. 223-225.

"Growing Trend to Early Retirement," *Compensation Review 5* 1 (1973) pp. 62-65.

Gustafson, T.A. "Early Retirement and the Labor Market Dynamics of Older Workers," Yale University Graduate School.

Haber, William, Ferman, Louis A., and Hudson, John. *The Impact of Technological Change: The American Experience* (Kalamazoo, 1963) pp. 47 ff.

Hamblin, W.H. "Mandatory Retirement and Dismissal in Institutions of Higher Learning," *Journal of The College and University Personnel Association 27* 2 (1976) pp. 1-15.

Harne, E.D. "Early Retirement is Possible," *Journal of Extension 15* (1977) pp. 23-25.

Haynes, S.G., McMichael, A.J., and Tyrsler, H.A. "Survival After Early and Normal Retirement," *Journal of Gerontology 33* 2 (1978) pp. 269-278.

Heard, John N. "Is Bigger Business Better? Not at First of Tulsa," *Pension World 13* 11 (1977) pp. 25-26.

Hodgens, Evan L. "Key Changes in Major Pension Plans," *Monthly Labor Review* (July 1975) pp. 22-27.

Hopkins, D.S.P. "Faculty Early-Retirement Programs," *Operations Research 22* 3 (1974) pp. 455-467.

"How IBM Avoids Layoffs Through Retraining," *Business Week* No. 2406 (1975) pp. 110-112.

Howard, E. "Mandatory Retirement—Traumatic Evidence of Age-Discrimination," *Trial 13* 11 (1977) pp. 46-51.

"Is There Anything Magic About Sixty-Five," *Dun and Bradstreet Reports 24* 5 (1976) pp. 20-27.

"It's England's Turn at Royal Dutch Shell," *Fortune 45* 2 (1977) pp. 20-24.

Jacobson, D. "Rejection of the Retiree Role: A Study of Female Industrial Workers in Their 50's," *Human Relations 27* (1974) pp. 477-492.

Jaslow, P. "Employment, Retirement and Morale Among Older Women," *Journal of Gerontology 31* (1976) pp. 212-218.

Johnson, L. and Strother, G. "Job Expectations and Retirement Planning," *Journal of Gerontology 17* (1962) pp. 418-428.

Jonas, Karen. "Factors in Development of Community Among Elderly Persons in Age-Segregated Housing: Relationships Between Involvement in Friendship Roles Within the Community and External Social Roles," *Anthropological Quarterly 23* 2 (1979) pp. 29-38.

Kandel, R.F. and Heider, Marion. "Friendship and Factionalism in a Tri-Ethnic Housing Complex for the Elderly in North Miami," *Anthropological Quarterly 23* 2 (1979) pp. 49-59.

Kell, D. and Patton, C.V. "Reaction to Induced Early Retirement," *Gerontologist 18* 2 (1978) pp. 173-179.

Kinzel, R. "Resolving Executives' Early Retirement Problems," *Personnel 51* 3 (1974) pp. 55-63.

Kolko, Gabriel. *Wealth and Power in America* (New York, 1962) pp. 48-51.

Kolodrubetz, Walter W. *Multiemployer Pension Plans Under Collective Bargaining* (Spring 1960), Bureau of Labor Statistics Bulletin 1326, 1962.

Kossoris, Max D. "Early Retirement," *Industrial Relations 4* 3 (1965) pp. 1-14.

Kottke, M.W. "Economic Growth Processes, Investment Strategies, and Environmental Quality Compatibility," University of Connecticut, Agricultural Experiment Station, Agricultural Economics.

Kramer, Robert and Barron, Jerome A. "The Constitutionality of Removal and Mandatory Retirement Procedures for the Federal Judiciary: The Meaning of 'During Good Behavior'," *George Washington Law Review 35* 3 (1965) pp. 455-472.

Kreps, Juanita. "Economics of Aging: Work and Income Through the Lifespan," *American Behavioral Scientist 14* 1 (1970) pp. 81-90.

Kroll, Arthur H. "Funding Employee Benefits Through a Section 501(c) (9) Trust—The Magic and the Mystery," *Review of Taxation of Individuals 2* 3 (1978) pp. 250-253.

Larkin, A. "Constitutional Attacks on Mandatory Retirement-Reconsideration," *UCLA Law Review 23* 3 (1976) pp. 549-579.

Lederer, V. "Will Congress Put Mandatory Retirement Out to Pasture?" *Administrative Management 38* 9 (1977) pp. 11-12.

Lehman, Harvey. *Age and Achievement* (New York, 1953).

Louvier, V. "The Fight Over Mandatory Retirement: How Old Is Old?" *Nation's Business 66* 3 (1978) pp. 48-54.

Lowenthal, M.I. and Berkman, P.M. *Aging and Mental Disorder in San Francisco* (San Francisco, 1967).

Mace, M.L. "Designing a Plan for the Ideal Board," *Harvard Business Review 54* 6 (1976) pp. 20-30.

Mancusco, T.F., Sanders, B.S., and Fuqua, P.A. *Disability and Mortality as Measures of Cancer.* The University of Pittsburgh, School of Public Health (1973).

"Mandatory Retirement Hearings in New York State," *Industrial Gerontology* (Fall 1974) pp. 13-21.

Manion, U. Vincent. "Issues and Trends in Pre-Retirement Education," *Industrial Gerontology* (Fall 1974) pp. 13-21.

Maule, H.G. "The Work of Industrial Psychologists in the Central Labour Institute, India," *Human Factors 10* 6 (1968) pp. 629-632.

McCaughey, Robert A. "The Transformation of American Academic Life: Harvard University 1821-1892," *Perspectives in American History 8* (1974) pp. 239-332.

McMahon, C.A. and Ford, T.R. "Surviving the First Five Years of Retirement," *Journal of Gerontology 10* 2 (1955) pp. 212-215.

Mellman, Richard J. "The Other Side of the 501 (c)(9) Story," *Pension and Welfare News 9* 6 (1973) pp. 45-53.

"Memo: A News Digest for Managers," *Administrative Management 38* 9 (1977) pp. 11-12.

Meyer, M. "Early Retirement," *Conference Board Record 9* 3 (1972) pp. 62-64.

Mihovilovic, Miro A. "The Status of Former Sportsmen," *International Review of Sport Sociology 3* (1968) pp. 73-96.

Milam, E.E. and Crumbly, D.L. "How to Integrate Deferred Compensation Benefits Into a Client's Estate Plan," *Estate Planning 5* 2 (1978) pp. 72-80.

Miles, William C. "ERISA—Factors to Consider in Administering Employee-Benefit Plans," *The Magazine of Bank Administration 52* 7 (1976) pp. 39-41.

Morrison, Malcolm H. "The Myth of Employee Planning for Retirement," *Industrial Gerontology* (Spring 1974) pp. 23-31.

Mousin, C.B. "Mandatory Retirement and Age-Discrimination-in-Employment-Act of 1967," *University of Illinois Law Forum 3* (1977) pp. 927-952.

Naiman, Robert M. "Selection of Investment Media by Qualified Employee Benefit Trust," *Taxes 51* 11 (1973) pp. 669-679.

Neugarten, Bernice L. "The Rise of the Young-Old," in Gross, Ronald, Gross, Beatrice, and Seidman, Sylvia, *The New Old: Struggling for Decent Aging* (New York, 1978) pp. 47-49.

Odell, Charles E. "The Case for Early Retirement," *Industrial Relations 4* 3 (1963) pp. 15-28.

O'Meara, J.R. "Retirement," *Across the Board 14* 1 (1977) pp. 4-8.

O'Meara, J.R. "Will Mandatory Retirement Be Outlawed," *Conference Board Record 13* 5 (1976) pp. 6-7.

Orbach, Harold. *Trends in Early Retirement* (Ann Arbor, 1969) pp. 14-33.

Orbach, Harold. and Tibbitts, Clark, eds. *Aging and the Economy* (Ann Arbor, 1963)

Palmore, Eardman. "Retirement Patterns Among Aged Men: Findings of the 1963 Survey of the Aged," *Social Security Bulletin 27* 8 (1964) pp. 3-10.

Palmore, Eardman. "Why Do People Retire?" *Aging and Human Development 2* (1971) pp. 269-283.

Parker, Donald F. "The Design and Analysis of an Expectancy Theory Model for Predicting Early Retirement," *Dissertation Abstracts International 35* 7-B (1975) p. 3636.

Parks, Richard W. and Barten, Anton P. "A Cross-Country Comparison of the Effects of Prices, Income and Population Composition in Consumption Patterns," *Economic Journal 83* 331 (1973) pp. 834-852.

Parnes, Herbert S., *et al. The Pre-Retirement Years* Volume 4. *A Longitudinal Study of the Labor Market Experience of Men,* U.S. Department of Labor, Manpower Research and Development, Monograph No. 15 (Washington, 1975).

Patton, Carl V. "Early Retirement in Academia: Making the Decision," *Gerontologist 17* (1977) pp. 347-354.

Pepper, C.D. "Mandatory Retirement," *Vital Speeches 43* 21 (1977) pp. 651-653.

Pepper, C.D. "Representative Pepper Speaks Out on Home Health-Care and Mandatory Retirement," *Geriatrics 33* 5 (1978) p. 27.

Peretti, P.O. and Wilson, R.C. "Voluntary and Involuntary Retirement and Their Effects on Emotional Satisfaction," *International Journal of Aging and Human Development 6* 2 (1975) pp. 131-138.

Plutchok. R. "Early Retirement," *Harvard Business Review 53* 6 (1975) p. 172.

Polhemus, C. "State Mandatory Retirement Upheld," *Monthly Labor Review 99* 10 (1976) p. 44.

Pollman, A.W. and Johnson, A.C. "Resistance to Change, Early Retirement and Managerial Decisions," *Industrial Gerontology 1* 1 (1974) pp. 33-41.

Postman, Harold. "International Aspects of ERISA," *Pension and Profit-Sharing Tax Journal 2* 2 (1978) pp. 178-183A.

Pyron, H. Charles and Manion, U. Vincent. "The Company, the Individual, and the Decision to Retire," *Industrial Gerontology 4* (1979) pp. 1-11.

Quinn, J.F. "Microeconomic Determinants of Early Retirement: Cross Sectional View of White Married Men," *Journal of Human Resources 12* 3 (1977) pp. 329-346.

Quinn, J.F. *The Microeconomics of Early Retirement: A Cross-Sectional View,* unpublished report prepared for the Social Security Administration (Washington, 1975).

Quirk, D.A. "Public Policy Note—Supreme Court and Mandatory Retirement," *Industrial Gerontology 2* 4 (1975) pp. 301-303.

Rappaport, A.M. "Prepare for World of Post-65 (and Early) Retirement," *Harvard Business Review 56* 4 (1978) pp. 6-7.

Reno, Virginia. "Incidence of Compulsory Retirement Policies," *Reaching Retirement Age,* Social Security Administration, Research Report No. 47 (Washington, 1976) pp. 53-64.

Reno, Virginia. "When Men Stop Working Before Age 65," *Reaching Retirement Age,* Social Security Administration, Research Report No. 47 (Washington, 1976) pp. 41-51.

Riley, Matilda White and Foner, Anne. *I Aging and Society,* Russell Sage Foundation; *An Inventory of Research Findings* (1968); Riley, Matilda White, Riley, John W., Jr., and Johnson Marilyn. *II Aging and the Professions* (1969); Riley, Matilda White, Johnson, Marilyn, and Foner, Anne, *III A Sociology of Age Stratification* (1972); Riley, Matilda White, "Age Strata in Social Systems," in Blinstock, Robert H. and Shanas, Ethel, eds., *Handbook of Aging and the Social Sciences* (1976).

Riley, P.A. "Abolishing Mandatory Retirement in Maine," *Aging and Work 1* 1 (1978) pp. 15-24.

Rose, Charles L. and Mogey, John M. "Aging and Preference for Later Retirement," *Aging and Human Development 3* 1 (1972) pp. 45-62.

Rosenblum, Marc. "The Last Push: From Discouraged Worker to Involuntary Retirement," *Industrial Gerontology* (Winter 1975) pp. 14-22.

Rosow, I. *The Social Integration of the Aged* (New York, 1976); Shanas, E. *Old People in Three Industrial Societies* (London, 1968).

Schier, R.F. "Raising Mandatory Retirement Age—Examining Consequences," *Intellect 106* 2391 (1977) pp. 214-216.

Schulz, J.H. "Economics of Mandatory Retirement," *Industrial Gerontology 1* 1 (1974) pp. 1-10.

Schneider, C. *Adjustment of Employed Women to Retirement,* Ph.D. Dissertation, Cornell University, 1964.

Schock, Nathan. *Trends in Gerontology* (Stanford, 1951).

Serwer, A.M. "Mandatory Retirement at Age 65—Survey of Law," *Industrial Gerontology 1* 1 (1974) pp. 11-22.

Shaifer, N. "Early Retirement," *Harvard Business Review 53* 6 (1975) p. 174.

Shearon, M.S. "Economic Status of the Aged," *Social Security Bulletin* (March 1938) p. 6.

Sheldon, A. *et al. Retirement: Patterns and Predictions* (Washington, 1975).

Shenk, Faye. "Career Indications Among Junior Officers," *USAF AFHRL Technical Report* No. 69-33 (1969) p. 12.

Sheppard, H.L. *The Greying of Working America: The Coming Crisis in Retirement Policy* (New York, 1977).

Sheppard H.L. "Issue of Mandatory Retirement," *Annals of the American Academy of Political and Social Sciences 438* (1978) pp. 40-49.

Sheppard, H.L. "Work and Retirement," in R.H. Binstock and E. Shanas, eds., *Handbook of Aging and the Social Sciences* (New York, 1976).

Sheppard, H.L. and Herrick, N.Q. *Where Have All the Robots Gone: Worker Dissatisfaction in the 70's* (New York, 1972).

Sills, David. *The Volunteers* (Glencoe, Il, 1958) pp. 253-268.

Skolnik, Alfred M. "Private Pension Plans, 1950-74," *Social Security Bulletin* (June 1976) pp. 3-14.

Slater, W.T. "Early Retirement—Some Questions and Some Options," *Journal of Higher Education 43* 7 (1972) pp. 559-566.

Sollee, William L. "Trust Agreements and Fiduciary Responsibilities Under ERISA," *Trusts and Estates 114* 11 (1975) pp. 778-823.

Squier, Lee W. *Old Age Dependency in the United States* (New York, 1912).

Stagner, R. "Affluent Society Versus Early Retirement," *Aging and Work 1* 1 (1978) pp. 24-31.

Stagner, R. "Boredom on the Assembly Line: Age and Personality Variables," *Industrial Gerontology 2* 1 (1975) pp. 23-44.

Streib, G. and Schneider, C.J. *Retirement in American Society* (Ithaca, 1971).

"A Strong Protest Against Forced Retirement," *Nation's Business 64* 7 (1976) pp. 14-15.

Sullivan, Donald E. "ESOPs: Panacea or Placebo?" *California Management Review 20* 1 (1977) pp. 55-61.

Sullivan, Donald E. "Never Too Old," *The Personnel Administrator 23* 6 (1978) pp. 54-58.

Sussman, M. "An Analytic Model for the Sociological Study of Retirement," in F. Carp, ed., *Retirement* (New York, 1972).

Taylor, A.L. and Coolidge, H.E. "Survey and Analysis of Early Retirement Policies," *Educational Record 55* 3 (1974) pp. 183-187.

"The Ax of Forced Retirement," *Business Week* 2501 (1977) pp. 38-39.

The Economic Aspects of Pensions: A Summary Report, National Bureau of Economic Research (1968).

"The Great Male Cop-Outs From the Work Ethic," *Business Week* 2509 (1977) pp. 156-159.

"Trust Assets Reach $403 Billion in 1972," *Trusts and Estates 113* 3 (1974) pp. 114-146.

Tyhurst, S.A., Salk, J.E., and Kennedy, D.E. "Mortality, Morbidity, and Retirement," *American Journal of Public Health 47* 3 (1957).

U.S. Bureau of Labor Statistics. *Digest of Selected Pension Plans, 1973 Edition* (including supplements), 1974-75.

Unger, H. "The Anti-Retirement Law: A Sign of Older People's New Political Clout," *Canadian Business Magazine 50* 11 (1977) p. 32.

Wagner, M.E. "Mandatory Retirement," *American Association of University Professors Bulletin 58* 3 (1972) p. 371.

Walker, J.W. and Price, K.F. "Impact of Vesting, Early Retirement, Rising Cost of Living and Other Factors on Projected Retirement Patterns—Manpower Planning Model," *Industrial Gerontology 1* 3 (1974) pp. 183-187.

Walker, J.W. "New Appeal of Early Retirement," *Business Horizons 18* 3 (1975) pp. 43-48.

Walker, J.W. "Will Early Retirement Retire Early," *Personnel 53* 1 (1976) pp. 33-39.

Weiss, J.A. and Warren, J.P. "Mandatory Retirement is Unethical and Inefficient," *Employee Relations Law Journal 2* 4 (1977) pp. 453-464.

"When Retirement Doesn't Happen," *Business Week* 2539 (1978) pp. 72-89.

Whitney, W. and Damroth, W.G. "Don't Call it Early Retirement," *Harvard Business Review 53* 5 (1975) pp. 103-108.

Williams, H.A., Pepper, C., and Roberts, H.B. "Should Congress Prohibit Mandatory Retirement of Workers Over Age 65?" *Congressional Digest 56* 11 (1977) p. 266.

Wirz, H.M. "Economics of Welfare: The Implications of Demographic Change for Europe," *Futures 9* 1 (1977) pp. 45-52.

Wood, N.J. "Challenge to Mandatory Retirement," *Labor Law Journal 27* 7 (1976) pp. 437-440.

Wood, N.J. "Mandatory Retirement and Equal Protection," *Labor Law Journal 28* 3 (1977) pp. 142-146.

Wood, V., Wylie, M., and Sheafor, B. "An Analysis of a Short Self-Report Measure of Life Satisfaction: Correlation with Later Judgments," *Journal of Gerontology 24* (1969) pp. 465-469.

Zalusky, J. "Shorter Work Years—Early Retirement," *AFL-CIO American Federationist 84* 8 (1977) pp. 4-8.

Zelan, J. "Options Relating to Voluntary Mid and Late Career Changes and Early Retirement for University and College Faculty," ABT Associates Inrcoporated (1977).